I Love Being a Woman

I Love Being a Woman

Patsy Clairmont

TYNDALE

Tyndale House Publishers, Wheaton, Illinois

I LOVE BEING A WOMAN

Library of Congress Cataloging-in-Publication Data
Clairmont, Patsy.
    I love being a woman / Patsy Clairmont.
        p.   cm.
    "Focus on the family."
    ISBN 1-56179-678-6
      1. Women in the Bible.   2. Christian women—
Religious life. I. Title.
    BS575.C54   1999
    220.9'2'082—dc21   99-35717
                                 CIP

A Focus on the Family book published by
Tyndale House Publishers, Wheaton, Illinois.

Editor: Janet Kobobel Grant
Cover design: Al Eiland
Cover photos: Scott Gibson
Interior illustrations: Carol Porter

Printed in the United States of America

99 00 01 02 03 04 05 06 / 10 9 8 7 6 5 4 3 2 1

to the woman
who not only taught me to love the lace of my femininity
but also to love the Lord who designed me,
my mom, Rebecca Ann McEuen

Contents

Acknowledgments

My husband has the amazing knack of making me laugh even when I don't want to. That aggravating gift has helped us both survive the ups and downs of book projects. When my eyes cross, my brain freezes, and I slump over my computer, Les scoops me up and takes me to dinner. Thank you, Les, for that and for the many other kind things you do to make my life easier, sweeter, and richer. And oh yes, funnier.

I thank my office staff, who also just happen to be my family—my son Jason; his wife, Danya; and my son Marty. Each of you helps me in a myriad of ways both practical and personal. I love that you all are an important part of what I do. Your expertise enhances my ministry efforts and your involvement blesses me.

My California buddies, Virginia Lukei and Jan Frank, remind me of God's love through the quality of their friendships with me. Lana Bateman's listening ear and praying heart help to steady me in this topsy-turvy world. These friends cause my heart to celebrate more deeply our wonderful feminine design. Thank you, my chums.

I travel with six exceptional women doing conferences: Mary Graham, Barbara Johnson, Marilyn Meberg, Luci Swindoll, Sheila Walsh, and Thelma Wells. These outrageous troopers have highlighted for me why I love being a woman. Thank you for exemplifying what it means to live life to its fullest.

Thanks to Focus on the Family and Tyndale House's joint effort, I have been allowed to share my heart. I specifically thank my bosses, Al Janssen and Doug Knox. Why, you guys aren't even bossy. Better yet, you are both gentlemen. Speaking of gentlemen, Larry Weeden is a joy to work with. He listens well, and he cares deeply. Thank you, Edie Hutchinson, for being a champion on my behalf and for all your energetic efforts.

If I were to spotlight one woman who has made significant contributions to making my writing dream come true, it would have to be my editor, Janet Kobobel Grant. She has been a tutor, a cheerleader, and an esteemed friend. I value her insights, I trust her judgment, and I respect her character. She is a woman worth knowing.

An Invitation

Hold onto your pantyhose, honey. We are about to investigate the ever-changing dynamics of being a woman. It will be like surfing, as we catch the crest of women's waves of emotions, plunge headlong into our exploding hormones, and ride the current of our demanding schedules.

A woman's world is anything but static—and gratefully so. We gals don't want moss growing over our path, but we don't want to feel as though we're being experimented on to see how far we stretch before popping either. Zing!

We're constantly trying to find balance in this head-over-heels world and to discover how to invest our energies wisely. As women today, our options are endless yet our life spans are restrictive. Time: our friend and our opponent. Whew! I'm grateful my times are in His hands.

One of God's sweetest gifts to women is their friendship with other women. I've been blessed with a plethora of comrades who have added richness to my life with their wit and wisdom. One of these gals is my lifelong friend Carol Porter. We have been cronies for many a year and have more memories than sense. When we were children, she and I planned to one day do books together. Carol was to be the artist, and I would be the author. Lo and behold, here we are 48 years later, and we know we'd better hurry because our hot flashes seem to be singeing our brain cells.

So recently Carol employed her artistic pen, and I added a twist of my humor, to come up with two characters, Tilly and Toodles, who represent us and, we believe, a gazillion other women. You'll see the "girls" pop up throughout this book as a reminder that you aren't alone in your struggles and frustrations. Honey, this topsy-turvy duo has been there and done that.

Also, Tilly and Toodles represent the lasting value of friendship. We hope these two gals give you a chuckle and remind you to appreciate and applaud the other women in your life.

Now, join Tilly and Toodles as they saunter off to grin, guffaw, and groan over the joys and—uh—jumble of being a woman. Don't you love it?!

1

Stretch Marks:
Sarah and Hagar

♥♡♥

hat is it about us women and our rubber-band emotions? It seems we accumulate wads of rubber bands inside of us and then become snippy and snappy. Consider Sarah and Hagar, who are congenially connecting one moment and flinging paper wads across the office at each other the next.

Their relationship started out, as many do, in the workplace. Sarah was boss, and Hagar was an attentive employee. But when Sarah gave Hagar a "promotion," their connection snapped. Evidently Hagar's job change changed her. She began to swell with pride, both her head and her tummy. Sarah's rubber bands tightened up with resentment toward Hagar until Sarah actually took potshots at her. Hurt and afraid, Hagar ran away.

What a mess! Hagar was jobless, homeless, single, and with child. To make matters more confusing, her boss's husband, at Sarah's insistence, fathered Hagar's unborn child. Holy rubber bands! No wonder everyone was so tense.

Sarah's emotional longings for a child evidently overtook

her good judgment, and she opted to expedite the divine plan for her life with her own bright ideas. But she wasn't prepared for the consequences, including Hagar's arrogant 'tude ("Nah, nah, I got pregnant before you did"), which made childless Sarah bonkers.

The Lord Himself sent runaway Hagar back to harsh Sarah. (That had to be scary and humbling.) Hagar returned with a new attitude. Hmm, or was Hagar just less obvious about her feelings in the workplace? Repression works . . . for a while. (Ask me.)

We don't hear any more about Hagar until her son, Ishmael, and Sarah's son (yep, she gave birth), Isaac, have a skirmish. Either Ishmael picked up on his mom's 'tude toward the boss or he just naturally fell into his own, but Ishmael decided to tease little half brother Isaac. Uh-oh, Ish. Bad choice.

Mama Sarah overheard Ishmael, and her rubber bands tangled into a wad of hysteria. Why, how dare that boy, that son of Hagar, bad-mouth Sarah's only child! Swinging her emotions around like a rubber-band lasso, she demanded that Hagar be booted—bag, baggage, and boy—from the camp . . . forever.

Zowie! Remind me never to offend Sarah! (Perhaps the constant visual of Hagar and Ishmael, reminding Sarah of how she allowed her ragged emotions to run ahead of God's plan, was just too much for her.)

We see a wide range of emotions in Sarah and Hagar's story, from warm, fuzzy acceptance all the way to get-out-of-my-face rejection. We hear Sarah laugh (Genesis 18:12) when she should have been learning, and we see Hagar prance when she should have been praying (Genesis 16:4). Impatience, jealousy, envy, and spitefulness all appear to be parts of their plight. We note the "girls" tugging on each other's rubber bands until, alas, Sarah's snaps.

If I could chat with Sarah and Hagar, I feel the two of them would understand me because I, too, have run amok when my feelings have been my guiding light instead of He who is the Light of the world. I'm still sportin' stretch marks from times when others have snagged my emotions and I have yanked back—hard—in response. And from times when I have been the antagonizer, causing others to wad up. Impatient, jealous, envious, and spiteful—yep, been there, done those.

What is it about us women and our rubber-band emotions? Truth be known, ladies, we are in this emotional flurry together. We are capable of going from fearful to flaunting to frenzied, and everything in-between. And I think it's time to talk. So join me as we have a confab on the wealth and health of our emotional makeup.

2

Emotionally Wealthy

❤❤

"They will feed in rich pasture on the mountains."
(EZEKIEL 34:14)

Synonyms: rich, affluent, prosperous

I love being a woman! I celebrate my femininity. I appreciate lovely items, soft surroundings, poetic verbiage, romantic trysts, finger-long lace, tea parties, floral bouquets, and shopping until my Rockports rot. I'm thrilled to have Eve qualities that set me apart from the Adams of this world. I prefer being the main nurturer and cheerleader of humankind. I take delight in the distinctive differences, in our feminine nuances that add to a woman's mystery and appeal. I'm pleased I'm considered huggable, reliable, and pleasurable.

I'm proud that history proves us gals to be competent, courageous, innovative, and invaluable. I stand taller to be named with those who have gone before us, from Old Testament Deborah and Ruth to New Testament Lydia, from Florence Nightingale to Corrie ten Boom. We have rocked cradles, ruled nations, and succeeded as entrepreneurs. We have successfully encouraged men and children on to their personal victories. Yes, yes, I do love being a woman.

Not that we girls don't also have unique challenges that

range from inconvenient to downright devastating. Take emotions, for example. Oh, please, take some of my emotions. Trust me, I have enough to share. In fact, sometimes my emotional wad has a way of spewing in all directions. These tangled eruptions leave me and others wondering, "What's going on?" How could the sweetheart, the mommy, the caregiver, the soft shoulder, the counselor also be Ms. Vesuvius?

Yes, our emotions can wreak a path of destruction. But we can avert being blown apart and blowing others away by our emotional wealth. First, though, I'd like to ask you a few questions.

What are you feeling right now? Can you count your emotions? How many different ones can you name?

Let me help. Perhaps you're feeling stable, content, and calm. (Wait a minute; is stable a feeling or a condition?) Maybe you are flighty, flaky, and forlorn. (Hmm, now are those feelings or behaviors?) Today you may find yourself functioning with peace, joy, long-suffering, and gentleness. (Hold everything! Aren't those fruit, as in fruit of the Spirit, and not emotions?) Yikes! No wonder we sometimes have problems expressing how we feel when we can't even define it.

We do know emotions emote. Or they should. They ought to be at our disposal to allow us to respond on a feeling level to life. They help us vent—positive emotions need venting as well as negative ones. For instance, I love Christmas, yet the holidays are emotionally complex for me. I begin the season feeling like a ribboned gift and finish feeling like the discarded wrappings under the tree. But I've noticed that when I avail myself of my emotional vents (more about these later), they serve as outlets for surviving Christmas without blowing a gasket. (Gasket blowing, unlike glass blowing, is so unattractive.)

We seem to have a gazillion more negative emotions than positive ones. Ever notice that? On the positive side we have love, joy, and peace (and their derivatives). In the negative column we have hatred, anger, bitterness, depression, disappointment, hurt, frustration, despair, sadness, fear, loneliness…

It appears the negative emotions, like bad guys, are ganging up on us. Does this mean we can't win? Or that we will always be overwhelmed or ambushed by our own emotional makeup? In the pages ahead we will consider our emotional options, especially for days when our feelings have crowded us against a rock and a hard place.

Rocks and hard places are things this cracked pot knows about, for I was held hostage by my rowdy emotions for a number of years. In fact, as a young adult I was housebound, an agoraphobic. I was paralyzed with fear, perplexed by guilt, and pursued by anger. Not an attractive trio, but one that many of us chum with as though we have no choice. I have learned we do have a choice; actually, it's more like a career because emotions are a full-time function in our lives, and they take both time and maintenance. A snit fit doesn't just happen; you have to nurture a lot of emotions to work up a good one.

You will note that the overriding theme of this book is emotions, even though the main topic is womanhood. I personally find it difficult to speak of one without the other. And I'm pleased that is true. I haven't always been delighted that emotions and womanhood are so tightly interwoven. And I still have shaky moments that leave me feeling emotionally tattered and wanting to have Goodwill drop by to pick up a sack of extra feelings I could live without. Overall, though, my emotions have become an exquisite gift to my life. Let me tell you why.

3

Emotionally Healthy

"I pray . . . you may prosper and be in good health."
(3 JOHN 2)

Synonyms: fit, sound, vigorous

J remember as though it were yesterday the deep thrill of holding my firstborn son. Once his tiny body was nestled in my waiting arms, my life was never again the same. I traced his little ears with my finger and whispered words of love. I counted his fingers and toes, marveled at his long eyelashes, and giggled at the full crop of black hair that ran all the way down into the collar of his pajamas. I promised myself, as I surveyed this wee baby, that I would go to church and commit my life to the Lord. I knew upon seeing my son that there must be a God who cared for me. The miracle of that little life caused me to seek the Life- Giver, Jesus. So several weeks after Marty's birth, in a little white church on a country hillside, in front of a congregation of 35, I was born anew.

During my prayer that day, as I invited Christ to enter my heart, scales fell from my eyes. I didn't see the scales, but I saw the change. When I stepped out the church's door, I felt as if I were seeing the heavens and earth for the first time. The sun, which was more brilliant than I remembered, was like a spotlight showcasing the rich blues of the heavens. The sight caused my breath to catch as the azure sky stretched endlessly above the rich, emerald grass. And then there was the lake. Oh my, the lake. It shimmered like a thousand diamonds refracting rays of dancing light across the water. Nature seemed to celebrate my decision to follow the God of creation. I had never experienced His handiwork at such an emotional level as I did the night of my son's birth and the day of my rebirth.

Those memories replay in living color because they are encased in emotions. Emotions cause feet to dance, eyes to laugh, hands to clap, friends to giggle, enemies to hug, people to give, children to sing, and memories to reverberate with meaning. Our feelings can fill us, frighten us, fortify us, and fool us. Someone handed me a saying the other day that made me chuckle over all the emotions tangled up in it: "Four out of five voices in my head said to eat the chocolate pie."

Emotions are scary when they come bearing heart-wrenching pain, and yet they are exquisite when they arrive with deep, soul-rinsing joy. Herein lies our dilemma: If we give up one, we lose the other. We can't shut down pain without sealing out joy. We can't ignore heartache without missing out on blessed relief. We can't say no to negative feelings without also nixing positive feelings.

So what's a woman to do when emotions flood over her like Niagara Falls? Well, let me make a recommendation. Stop. Look. And yep, you got it, listen.

"Hey, Patsy, wait a minute. That's kindergarten stuff," you say.

Really? When is the last time your emotions felt as though they were running you over? Can you think of a time you wished you had thought before you leaped off your emotional curb right into relational traffic? And if you're anything like me, you've often regretted listening to the four internal voices jeering at you to eat the chocolate pie.

In the fifth grade, I was a member of the Service Squad at

my school. The squad was a girls' group sort of like the boys' Safety Patrol. Only we girls guarded the school halls and sidewalks while the boys safely guided kids across street corners. Being in the Service Squad was a great honor because it signified you were trained in safety and therefore responsible to watch over others and, when necessary, to report offenders (tattletale!) to the appropriate person in authority. What was emphasized to both the Service Squad and Safety Patrol? Yep. Stop, look, and listen. Three basic steps whether you're watching for oncoming traffic to avoid accidents, slowing down runners in the halls to avert collisions, or, I add, preparing for onslaughts of feelings to bypass emotional disaster.

The "stop" step in dealing with emotions is monumental for me. It has helped me sort out the difference between sense and nonsense. For years I allowed my emotions to make decisions for me. If I didn't feel like getting up in the morning, I'd sleep till noon. If I didn't feel like cleaning the house, I'd allow stuff to pile up. (There's nothing more visually disconcerting than to live with a stuff pile-er.) And if I felt down, I'd mope about in a blue funk, infecting the environment with my moodiness.

That behavior, girlfriends, was nonsense and needed to stop. I was allowing my emotions to do for me something God never designed them to do—to think. As my friend Marilyn Meberg says so succinctly, "Emotions don't have brains." Pause and think on that!

Emotions were designed to connect us to life and people. They weren't meant to be reasonable or rational. And they certainly weren't designed to replace brain cells. Our tendency is to rely on one or the other—emotions or brains—which leaves us either heady and heartless or needy and clueless.

We need to learn how to have good heads and big hearts, which won't happen by us sitting on our posteriors. In fact, emotionally healthy people get that way through the diligent efforts of looking and listening—looking for and listening to the Lord's counsel. His direction is for our protection mentally and emotionally, as well as relationally.

When I started to integrate Scripture into my thoughts and to respond to its guidance regardless of how emotionally unsteady I felt, I began to even out. Instead of living off my frayed nerves, I chose to strengthen my mind with truth and deepen my character with obedience. That meant, when I didn't feel like getting up in the morning, I did it anyway. At first it was like trying to move a beached whale (an indulgent spirit is a weighty matter). When I didn't feel like cleaning the house, I did it anyway, but not all at once. In time I dug passageways through the debris and eventually restored order to my home. And when my mood was dark and foreboding, I dragged one lead foot in front of the other until I found a path of light.

It's not easy to change, but it is possible. And with every step of change, little by little my emotions began to support my efforts and validate my worth. Doing the right thing daily adds up to feeling better about yourself.

Even my reputation with others (family and friends) gradually began to change. I went from pathetic to practical to—at times—even profound. Of course, I still have some pathetic times, but at least now it's not a full-time career. And as far as my profundity, I have found that if I offer others His words instead of my opinions, which I have semitrailer loads of, not only do I come off brighter, but we also all benefit.

For me to move from just being emotionally wealthy to being emotionally healthy, I had to stop playing unhealthy games with my rubber-band emotions (like expecting them to think for me). I, like Sarah, needed to look for wisdom beyond my understanding, which means not succumbing to the dictates of my faulty calculations. And I, like Hagar, needed to listen by responding to God's message for my life: "This is the way; walk ye in it."

Now, some of you may think you're already a stop-look-and-listen gal. You're up before the rooster crows, your home is Martha Stewart spiffy, and you regularly can be heard happily singing rousing choruses of "I'll Fly Away." I know not all women are bound by their emotions as I was, but I do believe we all have the potential to learn and grow.

In the pages ahead, we will cover many aspects of a woman's life and responsibilities. We will consider how our emotional wealth can be distributed in healthy ways. We will take note of our longings to make meaningful contributions to a world in need of a woman's touch, words, vision, thoughts, heart, and spirit. The Lord has created us with the capacity to be both delicate and courageous, to be certain yet teachable, and to be nurturing yet strong. In the following chapters let's stop, look, and listen to women who have gone before us, who have succeeded and failed: women like Abigail, Ruth, Esther, Deborah, Hagar, and Sarah—women like you and me. Let's learn from their rich legacy to us.

So let's examine and celebrate together our wonderful feminine design. Women gravitate toward and even flourish in sistership. Like the girls' Service Squad, we can help each other along. And when one loses her way or her rubber bands tighten up, together we can call on Jesus, the Person in authority, for guidance.

4

All Good Gifts: A Prayer

❤♡❤

*W*e recognize, Lord, that You make no mistakes, and therefore even our wealthy emotional makeup is part of Your exquisite plan for us. We are aware that You did not design our emotions to rule our lives, but to give us the capacity to feel love, safety, and connectedness. Even loss becomes important to feel, lest we become rigid and untouched by others' sorrows.

Help us, Lord, on our Sarah days, when we would squander the wonderful resources of our emotions on being vengeful. Instead, may we purpose to extend forgiveness toward the Hagars in our world and toward ourselves for the part we've played in creating dilemmas.

Be with us in our Hagar moments, when we would puff up with arrogance and then hide in shame. May we remember to have a heart of gratitude, for all good gifts are from You.

We know our sister Sarah had wadded-rubber-band days, but she had many good days as well, days in which we clearly see Your protective hand guiding her life. And we can follow Hagar's sandal prints into the desert, where she knelt and prayed and You generously provided for her. Thank You that You help us throughout all our emotion-packed days. Amen.

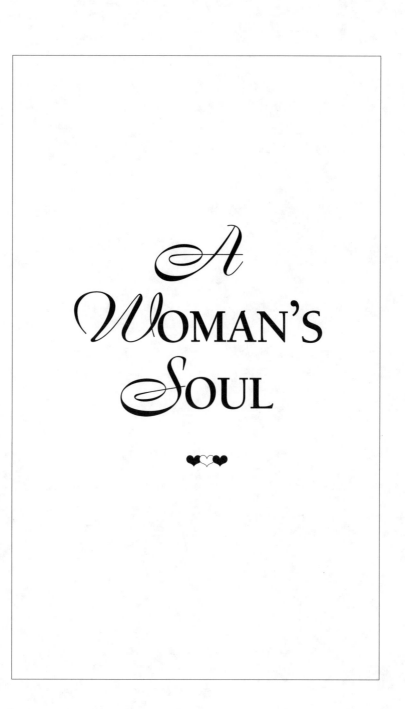

A Woman's Soul

5

Soul Food:
Abigail

❤♡❤

I think Abby (of 1 Samuel 25) may be the first person to offer a roadside deli. I know the Lord previously had cooked up a little heavenly hash (manna) to rain on the wandering parade of Israelites. Later we have Elijah, who ate on a wing and a prayer; a widow whose unending oil took the creaks out of hunger pangs; and I haven't forgotten the little lad whose fishy offering hooked a school of people. But I think Abigail was the first woman to take her food act on the road, a virtual meals on wheels. And one with food for the soul as well as the stomach.

Abigail offering others her food isn't what impressed me. But whom she fed and the way she did her presentation were exquisite. She makes me sing another chorus of "I love being a woman," what with her sensible soul and her wise ways.

But I'm ahead of myself; let me back up. Abigail was married to a fool. No fooling. Nabal was a first-class fellow with absolutely no class. He was wealthy in money and poverty-striken in people skills. He was both greedy and seedy. For Nabal planted seeds of disrespect and hatred in all those around

23

him. And when the miser offended David and his band of men with his unwillingness to share his bounty, Nabal brought about his own season finale.

You see, David's men had faithfully watched over Nabal's workers, protecting them and their flocks in the countryside from marauding bands of preying (not praying) men. But when the time came to stew the ewe, Nabal refused to share his food or table with David's crew. Nabal really was foolish, for everyone knows you don't get in the way of a famished man, much less four hundred hungry he-men—at least not without getting mangled. But that's what the ol' boy did. He locked up his pantry and his heart, pulled out a pint of Nabal's Numbing Nectar, and proceeded to get sloshed in the name of celebration. Oh, foolish one.

In the meantime, Abigail had been alerted by a servant, who knew Abigail was both approachable and wise, that David and his provoked posse were on their way. So Abby shifted into high-gear hostess mode. This situation required more than adding a few extra veggies to the pot; this was a far bigger brew. In fact, Nabal, his family, and his servants were all to be brewed up together. For David had vowed that Nabal and every male under his supervision would die that day for Nabal's narcissistic ways.

Abby opened her pantry and her heart as she picked out enough grub to feed a buffalo herd. The groceries were then packed onto a deli of donkeys that caravanned their way toward the approaching David. Abigail boarded her own donkey in an attempt to intercept tragedy. Now imagine this scene: 401 sworded, starving, incensed fugitives bent on murderous revenge (holy fig tree!) approaching one itsy-bitsy gal with the gift of hospitality.

The earth shook beneath Abigail's donkey as the vengeful vigilantes neared her. But this soulful woman seemed unperturbed by it all. She dismounted and lay prostrate on the ground before David. Then she did the most outrageous thing. She accepted responsibility for the entire fiasco that her surly husband had created. Hmm. Don't we call that codependent? But wait, see what happened next.

Once she had won David's ear, she filled it with undeniable truth. She asked David why he would want to stoop to her husband's behavior when David was anointed of the Lord while even Nabal's name meant "fool." She appealed to David's sense of integrity and destiny. Then she offered him food fit for a future king. Leave it to a woman to reach deep in her soul and come up with such a creative plan.

David chewed on her message and tasted the sweetness of her words. For this messenger had prevented him from making a bitter mistake. Indebted to her, David accepted her gifts and departed without bloodshed.

Abby then returned home to find Nabal too drunk to understand the severity of his situation. When he sobered up, she told him what had happened, and his heart turned to stone. Within 10 days, Nabal died.

David heard of Nabal's death and felt as though the Lord had settled the offense in His own immutable way. David then sent for Abigail and made her his wife, that he might royally repay her. Hmm. From a fool's home to a king's palace. What a journey!

I find anger intimidating regardless who is sportin' it, so I can't imagine facing an armed troop of mad men or women. Yet when we consider Abby's options of trying to reason with either a flaming fool or a raging, righteous man, her choice to lean toward David was wise. For a righteous person might come around to reason, but with a fool, there's not much hope. Our entrepreneurial sister Abigail was full of courageous hospitality and had stored a pantry full of resources in her soul to draw upon in time of need. Yes, I love being a woman!

6

Hospitable

♥♡♥

"Be hospitable to one another without complaint."
(1 Peter 4:9)

Synonyms: friendly, sociable, welcoming, warm

*I*t makes sense to me that the word *hospitable* is listed in the dictionary between *hospice* and *hospital*. Now, *hospice* means "a shelter or lodging for travelers, children, or the destitute." *Hospital*, of course, is a place that provides medical care for the injured or sick. And pillowed between those places of care is *hospitable*, the act of warmly welcoming guests and the ability to have an open, charitable, and receptive mind.

We see these qualities—openness, charitableness, and receptivity—demonstrated in Abigail's behavior as she brought her "guests" their meals on wheels, which she did with humility and grace. Her expression of hospitality foreshadowed her royal future, when that quality would come in about as handy as her full pantry.

Speaking of meals on wheels, such treats have intersected my path while I have been on the road traveling and speaking. These meals have helped make my journeys more memorable and hospitable. I promise you that, when you are out on the highways and byways, restaurant fare soon becomes wearisome.

Menus begin to take on a commonness that can lead to mental indigestion (hic). Excuse me. So to have someone open her pantry for you is impressive and appreciated. Take, for instance, the Franks . . .

My husband, Les, and I were attending a Christian Booksellers Association convention in Anaheim, California. Our friends Don and Jan lived near the hotel where we were staying, and they suggested we join their family for dinner one evening. We accepted and looked forward to visiting them and partaking of a home-cooked meal.

At the appointed hour, Don picked us up at the hotel. When we arrived at their home, Don turned the doorknob, only to find it locked. He looked at us as if he were surprised, then he rang the doorbell and stepped back. The door opened, and Jan greeted us in formal, maître d' mode. With a wave of her arm, she invited us to enter. Unsure of what was going on, we stepped into the living room with cautious interest. Then we stopped in our tracks.

The dining area was illuminated with candlelight and tiny white lights that were draped about the curtains and furniture. The flickering candles and soft music drew us to the table. It was covered with a linen tablecloth and adorned with china, silver, and stemmed goblets. The big surprise was not that they were using their finest wares for guests, but that the table was set for two. And sitting in front of the dinner plates was a large, framed picture of Les and me on our wedding day. Now, how did they get that?

Our thirty-fourth wedding anniversary was that day. We hadn't exactly forgotten it, but because of our demanding schedule, remembrance of the occasion was only a flicker in our minds. Obviously, the Franks had given it more consideration than we had.

They seated us and then disappeared through a blanket-covered doorway into the kitchen. Moments later, their lovely teenage daughters, Heather and Kelly, appeared and presented us with menus, filled our water glasses, and offered to take our orders.

Outside their kitchen, Don had the grill going to prepare our entrées while Jan and the girls prepared the rest. What a dining extravaganza! What an unexpected treat! What a demonstration of creative hospitality!

Truth be known, Les and I had been rather . . . well, how shall I say it . . . spatty prior to arriving at our friends' home. (Yes, after that many years you still spat.) But by the time our romantic anniversary interlude concluded with dessert, we were giggling sweethearts once again. The wedding picture softened our thoughts toward each other and brought back years of tender memories. (Jan had my secretary send her the picture from our wedding album, which was buried under old photographs in a trunk in our living room.)

When is the last time, as a family or an individual, you extended hospitality to someone on the road? Les and I will never forget that treasured time. And you know what? I don't think the Franks will, either. I have found that the more I put into an occasion, the more I take away from it. Trust me, the Frank family put a lot of themselves into that celebration.

Another time, after I had finished a women's conference in the Northwest, my hostess dropped me off at my hotel. She said someone had given her a gift for me and then added, "I think you're going to like it." She opened the back of her station wagon to reveal a beautiful sight. A tall, narrow, covered basket with Battenberg lace drizzling out the top and down the front beckoned me to pick it up and take it home. I acquiesced. I was so smitten with the outside appearance of my gift that I couldn't wait to get to my room to open it. So I sat down to explore the basket's interior in the hotel lobby.

The basket was layered in tea treasures. Each unfolding layer brought oohs and ahhs from my friends, who were seated nearby, and from me.

Strangers gave the gift to me. Imagine that. They were women from a tearoom, Angelina's, outside Portland, Oregon, who had read my tea book and wanted to send their greetings and make it possible for me to "do tea" on the road. They sent everything one would need: a polka-dotted teapot, cup, spoon, teas, scones, cookies, butter, champagne jelly, a tea cozy, and believe it or not, a gorgeous white rose. Also nestled in the basket was a tiny cream-velour purse containing a tea bag for travel. The presentation was elegant enough for a bride or a queen. I do love being a woman.

I can't tell you what that generosity did to refresh my exhausted soul. Like an infusion of fun and joy wrapped up in a hospitable spirit, the gift made me feel cared for while far from home. Thank you to the ladies of Angelina's, who exemplify the spirit of hospitality, being well disposed toward strangers.

For a while in our society, the term "random acts of kindness" drew interest and applause. And that was good. Yet I believe we are called to do more than randomly sow seeds of kindness. I believe we are admonished to continually extend ourselves to a road-weary world. Whether it's allowing someone to go ahead of us in a grocery line or on the freeway, or offering the neighborhood widow that extra piece of pie, little kindnesses offered regularly add up to big, heart-changing attitudes for all involved. A hospitable spirit is definitely a win-win proposition. Just ask Abigail.

7

Nurturing

❤❤❤

"As a nurse carries a nursing infant . . ."
(Numbers 11:12)

Synonyms: cherishing, maternal, strengthening

*R*emember the definitions from the last chapter for *hospice, hospitable,* and *hospital*? If we were to melt together the sheltering quality of a hospice, the physical caring of a hospital, and the welcoming warmth of hospitality, we would nudge up against the emotional essence of our next womanly attribute—nurturing. Yet nurturing is more than the sum of those three words, for to nurture is to promote development or growth in another; to bring up; to rear. It is to educate or train. It is to feed.

One might say Abigail offered her life as a hospice to David. She became a hiding place for him from his own anger, a refuge from the unfairness of life, a shelter from his insensibility. As David the traveler lodged in her wisdom, he found once again his sanity, his decency, and a sense of his nobility.

Many times women have been given soul-deep nurturing skills to assist life-weary men in getting back on track. We seem to be able to help them see past their steam so they can refocus their dream. This is no small contribution; I wouldn't want to see an account of history minus the powerful influence of women's lives in men's successes.

Abigail expressed hospitable ways as she extended courtesy and generosity to David and his thugs (1 Samuel 25:27). But she also was a hospital for David and his men when they were hostile and hungry. Nurse Abigail soothed their wounded pride, bound up their need to retaliate, and fed their starving bodies.

She taught by example what it means to be a nurturer, literally being willing to lay down her life for her family and workers. She encouraged David to grow into his crown by being a leader with compassion and vision.

Then this incredible woman blessed David. What a soul-soothing, nurturing thing to do, like a mother blessing her children. Listen in: "Should anyone rise up to pursue you and to seek your life, then the life of my lord shall be bound in the bundle of the living with the LORD your God" (1 Samuel 25:29).

I love the words "bound in the bundle of the living." I remember learning how to bundle my babies to keep them safe during our sometimes severe Michigan winters. I would carry my little ones close to my heart, protecting and warming them with my life. Abigail knew David would have those who would rise up against him in the future and that he already was on the run from King Saul, whose hatred for David was like a whipping winter wind. She understood David's need to be reassured during this cave-dwelling season of his life that God was near and had him safely tucked under His wings and close to His heart.

Then Abigail continued, "But the lives of your enemies He will sling out as from the hollow of a sling" (verse 29).

Not only was the blessing nurturing, but it also was brilliant. Who knew better than hotshot David the power of a slingshot against his enemies? Abigail fed David the truth about his past and his future all in one prayer. In this one verse she reminded him of God's power, provision, and protection. And she said in so many words, "Just as the Lord God caused Goliath to be slung to kingdom come, He can handle that fool Nabal and that jealous King Saul." Oh, the nurturing power of well-placed words.

Listen to David's response to Abigail: "Blessed be the LORD God of Israel, who sent you this day to meet me, and blessed be your discernment, and blessed be you, who have kept me this day from bloodshed and from avenging myself by my own hand" (verses 32-33). David recognized how blessed he was to have Abigail intercept him on the road with her nurturing presence.

Built into a woman's cells is a longing to invest herself lovingly and wisely into other's lives. We are instinctive nurturers. Our very design of having a womb and breasts shows we were created to nurture life. May we as women walk and talk as exquisitely as our sister Abigail.

She obviously prayed before she walked and thought before she talked. She was generous with her life to the point that she offered it for others, and wise enough to face anyone with the truth when called to take a stand. Yet her powerful words were set off with mercy and tenderness. She was quick to take responsibility and just as quick to pour out blessings on others. The soulful woman Abigail is a true heroine of the faith.

8

Approachable

♥♡♥

"Be devoted to one another . . . ; give preference to one another."
(ROMANS 12:10)

Synonyms: accessible, responsive, agreeable, open

*T*he word *approachable* makes me consider Christ's open-life policy. I can't think of anyone He cold-shouldered or refused entrance into His presence.

Oh, a few times He sidestepped trouble, and sometimes He sought out solitude. But generally speaking, the crowds freely sought Him out. Some people left His presence rapidly when they didn't want to hear the truth, but all were given access to Him. And what a lineup it was:

Pharisees—conniving religious leaders full of themselves

Tax collectors—notorious for cheating people

Prostitutes—women trapped in their sin

Lepers—abhorred by society

The demon-possessed—community castoffs

The desperate—individuals with personal agendas

Now, I have to confess, if a leper, a prostitute, and someone insane were headed toward me, I would duck into the dough-nut shop until they passed by. I'm not saying that's right; I'm just admitting my fallible makeup.

Perhaps you feel the same way. Not that we don't have compassion for them, but we often don't feel equipped to offer liberating solutions to their devastating issues.

Now wait; do we need to have all the answers to remain approachable? I think not. Actually, people who have all the answers get on most folks' nerves. So what does it take to be an approachable woman? Here are a few considerations:

• A willingness to accept people where they are . . . until they can take the next step. That kind of willingness is usually born out of personal growth and the recognition that we are all cracked pots. God is not partial but extends Himself to all.

Abigail obviously had established herself as approachable to her servants. She was not an employer who lorded her position over others. Servants, thugs, and kings were given the same consideration from this soul who extended herself to others.

• A willingness to listen; one who hears with her heart and answers when asked. That one is a toughie for me because my answers often fly out before I've fully listened. That tendency makes me store up assumptions, opinions, and defensiveness. And being full of those things can be lethal to one's maturity as well as one's relationships.

Abigail could have been offended when the servant said her husband was "such a worthless man that no one can speak to him" (1 Samuel 25:17). But she knew what her servant said was true, and a defensive spirit wouldn't save the people placed in jeopardy because of Nabal's haughty heart. Instead, her soul resonated with the truth the servant spoke, and her heart responded with generosity in the face of David's anger.

• A willingness to believe the best—not necessarily the best of people, but the best of God, who is at work in people's lives regardless how snarled the threads of their existence may seem. Scripture tells us that the heart of humankind is desperately evil, but the plan of God is to give us a future and a hope. As approachable women, we can help others see God's best.

Abigail reminded David of the future God had for him: "For the LORD will certainly make for my lord an enduring house, because my lord is fighting the battles of the LORD, and evil will not be found in you all your days" (1 Samuel 25:28).

It helps us to lift our own standard when we are given a glimpse of His great plans, doesn't it? Listen, girls. If you accept me where I am, hear my heart, and believe in God's best for me, not only are you approachable; you, dear ones, are my new best friends!

When Jesus allowed Himself to be approached by the masses and the messes, they left His presence new, whole, healed, heard, instructed, corrected, and gladdened. How are folks after they have encountered you?

9

Gregarious

♥♡♥

*"Two are better than one. . . . For if either of them falls,
the one will lift up his companion."*
(ECCLESIASTES 4:9-10)

Synonyms: companionable, cordial, amicable

*D*id you know that *gregarious* means "to form a group
with others of the same kind, as in a flock"? From just off the top
of my cranium, which in my case is a thin layer of fatty deposits,
I thought *gregarious* meant an outgoing, joyous person.

Of course, it does help to have a delightful disposition
when one is desiring to join a flock. People prefer to share their
pasture with those who have pleasant ways. I don't mean sac-
charin saints too sweet to swallow, but those whose nature is
centered in the Lord's Spirit. In fact, people flock to those folks
in hopes some of their winsome ways will rub off.

Like most women, I love flocks. I come from a small flock.
My parents had three little lambs over a period of 22 years. My
brother and sister and I were each like an only child during our
growing-up time. While many would be desirous of that opportunity, I longed for others to graze and huddle with on a daily
basis. So I was very big on joining groups, clubs, teams, and
other kids' large families. I even enjoyed being part of a clique
for its flocklike feeling. You can imagine the thrill I felt when I

gave my life to Christ and found I was now one lamb among many. I had been herded into a huddle where I stood shoulder to shoulder with those who listened for the Shepherd.

Over the years, the Lord has used His flock to strengthen me, comfort me, even protect me. But at times, some flock members have rubbed my wooly coat the wrong way, and I have wanted to renege on the group gathering—not the Shepherd, mind you, but I definitely could have done with fewer sheep in the pen. I'm grateful the Shepherd didn't leave it up to my discretion to decide who gets in. I would have turned some over to the wolves, but those sheep ended up being important to this dumb sheep's growth.

At other times I would have fallen had some sheep not sidled up to me to help me stand. Then there were the times in which I wandered off and fell, but the Shepherd righted me, and His sheep once again stood and grazed with me. Grazing with others who have an appetite for His Word is thrilling. I have a number of gregarious companions who, when we ruminate together, find it strengthens us all.

One of the wolves' tactics is to isolate a lamb and convince her she is all alone, hopelessly stuck in thorny thickets. But the truth is that every lamb has strayed at one time or another, and the Shepherd is ever near, willing to risk His all to retrieve His sheep.

Abigail was a gregarious shepherdess. She was watching after the flock (her servants) placed under her influence and went out on a limb (as a sacrificial lamb) to save her flock from ravenous wolves who would have devoured them. Shepherdess Abigail was also a sheep in need of a Shepherd's guidance, as she appeared all alone in her threatening predicament. The Good Shepherd, though, rescued her when He turned fiends into friends, a stoic into stone, and her pasture into a palace. He is ever near.

Abby saw the fallen state of her companions, and her soul felt concern for them. She knelt to lift them up. Sometimes when our friends or family are ensnared in sticky thickets, being on our knees—if not on our faces—is the best position before the King. Our King is also our Shepherd, and that truth comforts this little lamb. How about you?

Gregarious: belonging to a flock. Yes, I like that a lot.

10

Cooperative

"United in spirit, intent on one purpose."
(PHILIPPIANS 2:2)

Synonyms: harmonious, helpful, collaborative

J wonder, if we peeked into Abigail's pantry as she directed her servants in the preparation of the peace offering that she would take to David and his men, whether we would see, along with human fear, some divine excitement. I believe, by observing Abigail's behavior, that she was acquainted deeply with the Lord and His ways.

One doesn't suddenly act so courageously and speak so wisely without a history of faithful responsiveness deep down in one's soul. Even though her heart may have been pitter-pattering, I think her mind was rehearsing all the ways the Lord had protected and provided for her in the past. After all, you can't be married to a hard-hearted fool and not need regular divine intervention.

Yes, I believe Abigail, in those tense, life-threatening moments, remembered God's strong, loving hand upon her. And I believe she agreed to walk in cooperation with Him, even if that meant meandering into the path of her enemies. Otherwise, I don't believe she would have had the assurance and grace that so obviously clothed her.

Imagine the privilege that is ours to cooperate with the Creator of the world, He who designed the sun, moon, stars, planets, galaxies, seasons, tides, and weather systems to all coordinate and cooperate with His plans. As the song says, "He's got the whole world in His hands." That takes my breath away.

Moms especially are impressed, for we know how difficult it is just to coordinate our families enough on Sunday mornings to rush out the door on time for church services, much less have their cooperation. I can't even find socks to match or pantyhose without a run while He securely holds humankind's future.

It makes perfect sense that we would want to cooperate with the Lord . . . until He asks us to do something that makes no earthly sense. Of course, He already has warned us that His ways are not our ways (Isaiah 55:8). Yet we still want what He asks of us to be sensible. We would take refuge and find our safety in sensibility if He would let us.

I can't tell you how many times I've said, "Well, I'm sure glad His ways are different from mine because I would have botched things up." Of course, that's hindsight speaking, when I'm safely on the other side of an issue and His ways now make total sense. But in the midst of turmoil, when my vision is myopic, my stomach knotted, and my heart thumping out, "Born to lose, I've lived my life in vain," it's difficult to cooperate with God's mysterious plan.

That's why I'm so impressed with Abigail. Scripture tells us that when she heard the dire straits her household was in, she "hurried" to make preparations. And when she rode out to meet David and saw him approaching, she "hurried" to meet him. No sounds of resistance or reluctance, no whining, "Why me?" We don't hear her saying it isn't reasonable for an unarmed, solitary woman to go out and face a battalion of armed men. No, instead we see a spirit of cooperation, a willingness to do what needed to be done. And the results—the mysterious, breathtaking results—were that her enemies became her friends, her servants were spared, and Abigail's future was solidified. Why, it does my soul good just to think about the end of that story.

And it reminds me of the time I watched my little mama, at the age of 80, board an airplane with one small suitcase to begin a new life living with my sister and her family in Florida. I thought she was incredibly brave to go alone and to take so little. But Mom has a long history with the Creator of the universe, and she has learned to trust Him and cooperate with His plans.

What does it take to be a woman whose soul is so in touch with the Savior that she can be brave like Abigail and my mom, Rebecca? A pantry full of cooperation and a suitcase full of trust.

Abigail learned to be cooperative in the dailyness of life and then carefully stored those experiences on shelves she could reach. When the crisis came, she didn't hesitate but hurried into the thick of action with everything she needed. Rebecca left behind the security of all she had ever known to face the unknown, and she did it unencumbered.

When I see that Abigail took only food and my mama took only a small suitcase, I wonder if I wouldn't be better off if I carried less and cooperated more. After all, I could use some divine excitement in my life!

11

A Well-Stocked Pantry:
A Prayer

❤♡❤

*L*ord, we know it must not have been easy for Abigail to have lived and slept with thick-headed, hard-hearted Nabal. What a way to learn hospitality! Many times her soul must have been wounded by his caustic nature, embarrassed by his stinginess, and threatened by his anger. But You, Lord, rescued her just as certainly as if You had swept in on a white horse and ridden off with her to safety. Only You did it in Your time and in Your way instead of ours. You, Lord, changed a victimized woman into a valiant warrior.

And because of that, I'm not surprised to find that, instead of an army to influence David, you used an Abby. Instead of a fine white stallion, she arrived on a humble donkey. Instead of offering excuses, she became an example. And You, Lord, transformed the heart of a vengeful soldier into the heart of an honorable king.

Lord, some days we hear the thunderous hoofbeats of our enemies (our schedules, our co-workers, our finances, etc.) bearing down on us. May we find our souls hospitable enough to have our pantries well stocked with Your wisdom, and may we approach others with truth and in grace. And, Lord, may You find us hurrying to cooperate with You by fitting into Your mysteriously royal plan.

We as women want to have the soul-delighting attributes of an Abigail, for we fear that at times we may behave more like a thick-headed Nabal, unwilling to hear the truth and unwilling to change. Keep our hearts soft by Your regular visits in our lives. We open our heart's door wide to you; the welcome mat is out. Nurture us through Your Holy Spirit. We are in need of being bundled and drawn close. For when we have been close to You, we are prepared to be near others—even our enemies, but especially Your flock. Amen.

A
WOMAN'S
EYES

12

Strands of Faith: Ruth

❤︎❤︎❤︎

*Y*ou may want to place a magnifying glass next to the book of Ruth, for the details of this dazzling story are too elegant to risk missing. I have heard Ruth and the historical setting of her life compared to a pearl presented against a black velvet backdrop. Times then were spiritually—and therefore morally—bleak. Hmm, much like now. Ruth, despite the surrounding corruption in the land, chose to live admirably. Since I tend to be a group follower, I'm drawn in interest and desire to anyone who goes against society's flow to live a life of honor. In this section, "A Woman's Eyes," I want to examine for myself how this woman managed to walk faithfully despite devastating losses and painful changes.

Many events in Ruth's life, including her exemplary behavior toward her mother-in-law, Naomi, and toward the landowner Boaz, shine with her inner humility and integrity. The Lord's hand guided Ruth to find solace, solutions to her concerns, and shelter in her own home. Yet, one thing about Ruth that makes my heart skip a beat is that she was from a godless society. She wasn't raised to follow the one true God.

We don't know what convinced her to choose Yahweh's ways. Perhaps when she married Naomi's son, Ruth was exposed to the family's spiritual life and drawn to the God of Israel. Isn't it amazing and thrilling that someone so new to her beliefs in the Lord could live with such sensitivity to His leading?

We hear her incredible statement of faith when she pledges herself to the God of Naomi. Ruth's words, like a strand of pearls, gleam with covenant promise:

> Do not urge me to leave you or turn back from follow-ing you; for where you go, I will go, and where you lodge, I will lodge. Your people shall be my people, and your God, my God. Where you die, I will die, and there I will be buried. Thus may the LORD do to me, and worse, if anything but death parts you and me (Ruth 1:16-17).

If you don't find that breathtaking, I encourage you to lift your magnifying glass and take another gander; that or invest in trifocals. This is a newly converted, newly widowed young woman who has just given up all that she has ever known to follow her mother-in-law and her God into the unknown. Ruth leaves behind her husband's freshly dug gravesite, her family, her friends, her culture, and her homeland to live out her life in service to Naomi.

The thought of Naomi leaving Ruth fills Ruth's heart with such anguish that twice on the roadway leading to Bethlehem, she lifts up her voice and weeps as she pleads with her departing mother-in-law to allow her to follow. Have you ever thrown back your head and wept aloud at someone's departure? Has anyone done that at your farewell? Can you picture this clinging, wailing woman begging to follow you home? How would that make you feel? Frightened? Confused? Loved?

Well, finally Naomi concedes and allows Ruth to return with her to her homeland. Initially this daughter-in-law has little impact on her heavy-hearted mother-in-law, who feels as though her Maker's hand is set against her. All that changes, though, as Naomi experiences God's tenderhearted love through Ruth's life. Naomi had no way of knowing what the Lord had in store for her or what He would place in her arms to fill her aching heart.

Seldom does God allow us a sneak peek into our futures. Oh, He gives us wonderful promises and prophetic statements, but we don't know the ins and outs of His plans. I'd love to own a pair of holy binoculars so I could see what's coming.

Or would I? When I think of Naomi's life, the end was excellent, but the middle was excruciating. If I had been her and had seen through long-distance glasses that I would suffer the loss of my husband and sons, I don't think I would have had the strength to walk into that season.

No, on second thought, forget the binoculars. I'll stick with the life of faith, taking one step at a time and trusting the Lord to see me through, come what may. He "sees" so much better than I do, for He is our Alpha and Omega. I'm grateful that all our beginnings and endings, all our comings-in and goings-out, all our losses and all our gains, are in His sovereign care.

Ruth, this gleaming gem of a woman, somehow seemed to grasp the Lord's all-encompassing care for her future. With pearls of kindness and compassion draped about her, she proceeded to give her life away. Note that she didn't distribute herself frivolously but wisely, as God directed her steps. We will see in the pages ahead that Ruth's life was fruitful beyond her physical ability and certainly beyond her dreams.

13

Sensitive

❤♡❤

"When [they] heard about all the troubles that had come upon him, they set out from their homes and met together by agreement to go and sympathize with him and comfort him."

(JOB 2:11, NIV)

Synonyms: perceptive, receptive, tuned in, sympathetic

A downside exists in being sensitive, as is true with any good quality. If you take a strength to the extreme, it can become your worst nightmare . . . or someone else's. And we all probably know someone who is overly sensitive. You know, the one who leaves us tiptoeing through the tulips in our tutus as we attempt not to offend her.

Okay, okay. I confess that sometimes I'm the culprit. Not only am I delicately wired, but also at times I'm overwired. And when my wires cross, the results can be sizzling. I don't know how you cover your frayed wires, but my self-protective mode is to be sarcastic or distant, behaviors that are unattractive and ineffective. Actually, there is an effect, but it's a rather scorching one.

My definition of sarcasm is "hostile humor," like someone tickling you while simultaneously pulling your hair. Distancing: "a lonely existence." The habit of distancing oneself is similar to living on a slowly sinking island.

As I examine Ruth's behavior, I don't hear any sarcasm and

I don't see her withdrawing. Instead, her speech is fragrant with passion and thoughtfulness. I watch as she draws close first to Naomi and later to Boaz. At one point, when Ruth is pleading with her mother-in-law to be allowed to follow her, Naomi tells Ruth to go back to her own home and her own gods as Ruth's sister-in-law did. Oh my. Naomi must not have read the "Four Spiritual Laws."

Ruth could have allowed Naomi's words to offend her. She could have spun around in her sandals and retreated, leaving Naomi in Ruth's indignant dust. What a shame that would have been for them both. Instead, Ruth literally clings to Naomi, her beloved but bitter mother-in-law, until Naomi gives in to Ruth's request.

Imagine being strong enough and sensitive enough to shed offenses and cling to life. Case in point: Observe as Naomi first enters Bethlehem with Ruth. As the townspeople flock to greet them, Naomi says, "I went out full, but the LORD has brought me back empty" (Ruth 1:21).

Excuse me, Naomi, but what about Ruth? Doesn't she count? I feel offended for her, but Ruth gives no indication she internalizes Naomi's comment. I guess Ruth senses that her mother-in-law's words are the sounds of one with a crushed spirit. Ruth looks beneath her mother-in-law's words to Naomi's heart and understands the statements are about Naomi, not against Ruth.

How a person responds to pressure reminds me of a lovely container of spray sachet I have that sweetens the rooms in my home. According to the label, it is full of fragrance, yet in large letters are the words "Caution: contents under pressure." On a back panel are further warnings regarding problems if the contents become too heated or if someone tampers with the valve.

The Lord longs for His fragrance to be emitted through our lives, but some of us have allowed life's pressures to build up until we are potentially explosive. We have allowed slights to become fights, as our hurt heats up our anger. Then, instead of spraying, we are spewing—also known as being sarcastic—and stewing—also known as distancing. Scripture admonishes us to have our "senses trained to discern good and evil" (Hebrews 5:14). This training comes from internalizing God's Word, which fills us with healthy sensitivity. When lived out, that sensitivity releases to others the sweet fragrance of Christ.

Even though the pressure was extreme for Ruth, a new widow who had left behind all that was familiar, she still maintained a soft demeanor and tender tones. Yes, Ruth was responsive to her external surroundings because she was internally trusting the Lord to guide her every step. Oh, that I might see life through Ruth's eyes: full of sweet belief and sensitivity toward others rather than being caught up with *moi*.

14

Soft

*"My daughter, shall I not seek security for you,
that it may be well with you?"*
(Ruth 3:1)

Synonyms: mild, pliant, tranquil

We've all heard of people who are considered a soft touch . . . like my dad. As a child, I knew if I needed some money, he was the one to go to. I'm not talking a big chunk of change, but, say, the price of a new *Archie* comic book, a pack of Juicy Fruit gum, a bottle of Dr. Pepper, or a quarter's worth of foot-stompin' tunes on the jukebox. Now, if I was looking for a soft shoulder to cry on, I would go to my mom. It wasn't that Dad's shoulder was hard, but he was befuddled by my boo-hooing, whereas Mom just allowed me to wail.

My mom was also a soft touch. No, let me rephrase that. My mom had a soft touch. She fluffed pillows, smoothed sheets, cuddled babies, stroked hair, soothed brows, pampered pets, and embraced the brokenhearted with the touch of an angel. And my mom's heart was soft. I watched her weep many times with others who were in dire straits. Because Mom's tears were so plentiful, we used to tease her that we were going to hire her out as a professional mourner. Today I believe Mom's tears actually helped to keep our family's lifescape more tender.

I wonder if Ruth's tears were the beginning work of God in softening Naomi's grief-stricken life. Naomi's name meant "sweetness" or "pleasantness," but after the deaths of her husband, Elimelech, and sons, Mahlon and Chilion, she gave herself a new name: Mara, which means "bitter." It is no stretch for us to understand why a woman who had buried her husband and sons would feel bitter. Yet we also realize that to remain bitter would wither Naomi's soul and wilt those around her. Naomi went from a pleasant personality to a wretched one that would distance her from others, leaving her interior desolate, much like a coin that drops to the bottom of an empty well. Nothing is lonelier than hearing the echo of our own bitter words reverberate off the wall of our personal agony.

The word *soft* means "malleable, easily molded, not hard." Hmm, like clay on a pottery wheel. That seems to be the process both Naomi and Ruth were in as they left Moab and made their way toward Bethlehem; they were being remade in a way that pleased the Potter. Through the pressure of His sculpting hands, He began to smooth out the imperfections of bitterness and disappointment while He reshaped their characters and redesigned their future.

When Naomi journeyed toward Bethlehem, she headed in the right direction. She left her futility (trying to understand her losses) to walk toward her future (His ongoing plan for her life). Gradually, Mara's heart healed. The Lord lanced the bitterness of her soul with the generosity of His provisions and the softness of His healing presence.

I've observed how life's hardships have caused some women to become hard while others, like Ruth, have become soft. Not soft in the sense of weak, but soft-spirited, able to extend themselves in genteel ways.

My new friend Marilyn is that kind of gracious woman. She owns a tearoom decorated in simple elegance. Everything is white: tablecloths, dishes, candles, long-stemmed roses gracing the tables. Marilyn tells of how this feminine, soft surrounding has affected women who have visited for tea. One trio of ladies who had visited the parlor commented to Marilyn, "As we conversed in this lovely environment, we realized we've lost the lace in our lives."

It's easy in this fast-paced, sometimes hard-handed world to lose touch with the soft side of our feminine nature, the lacy part. Then we settle for basics and don't make the effort to tend to soft detailing, whether that be a tablecloth at dinnertime, a tatted handkerchief for teary moments, or a genteel answer spoken to a broken heart.

Ruth, a lacy woman on many levels, devoted herself to the needs of her grieving mother-in-law. Softly supportive, Ruth saw Naomi's pain and was there for her when she needed Ruth the most. So Ruth gently gave her life away.

Keeping that kind of demonstrated softness protects us and those around us against a hard, bitter existence. I want others to see that softness in me, and I hope to have eyes that see where to apply a bit of lace here and there to soften life's blows for others.

15

Kind

♥♡♥

"Be kind and compassionate to one another."
(EPHESIANS 4:32, NIV)

Synonyms: benevolent, gentle, agreeable

A fellow named John Watson said, "Be kind. Everyone you meet is fighting a hard battle." My heart resonates with that thought. But . . . have you noticed that some people seem more naturally kind by temperament?

I'm sad to say I ain't one of them. I'm not proud of that. In fact, at times I'm downright grieved by my feisty personality. I sizzle when I should serve, and I react when I should respond. I used to wish I was different. With crossed fingers, I hoped that in the night I'd be sprinkled in sweetness by, I dunno, perhaps the Sugarplum Fairy, or at least her second cousin Nutra-Sweetie.

But the truth is, hoping and wishing aren't going to produce kindness, for this quality is a fruit of the Spirit. That means the Lord is willing to work kindness into my heart if I'm receptive, and I must work out kindness with His empowerment. Fruitful hearts, though, must first be seeded if they are to be bountiful in enduring qualities. And the receptive heart is often one that has been broken, which then allows the seeds of kindness to take root at deep levels. This in-depth seeding ensures deep roots and sweet fruit.

Twice in Scripture Ruth is described as kind. Contained in her story are many examples of her daily commitment to being a thoughtful person. Ruth, according to her mother-in-law, had been kind to her deceased family and to Naomi. Later, Boaz, Naomi's relative, blesses Ruth for her kindness toward him.

When we consider the blustery season of Ruth's life, with multiple losses and dramatic changes, it's impressive to see kindness become a way of life for her. In contrast, Naomi, traumatized by her losses, becomes embittered and returns to Bethlehem empty and angry.

The bite of bitterness can be heard and felt in Naomi's remarks as she drags her heavy heart homeward. Her responses —not healthy or attractive—seem humanly reasonable when you weigh her catastrophic losses. The contrast of Ruth's kindly comments and behavior becomes even more striking when set against the backdrop of the two women's shared pain.

How must life have looked to Ruth that she could respond to it with open-heartedness and kindness rather than with a closed spirit and bitterness?

Recently I picked up a pear bearing a sticker that read, "Ripe when fruit yields to gentle pressure." The fruit borne in Ruth's life came out of extreme pressure as she walked through the death of her husband, brother-in-law, and father-in-law. Then she lost her homeland, friends, and family. How does a woman lose so much and become so kind?

When, Sister Ruth, was kindness sown into your heart?
Was it seeded by death, when your life broke apart?
Was it then that the seeds were watered by your tears,
Knowing your loss could bring long, bitter years?
What caused, Sister Ruth, the kindness to take root?

Was it the Gardener's care that protected the shoot?
For I see His fruit upon you like a clustered vine.
And I watch your broken life poured out like sparkling wine.
What caused, Sister Ruth, His fruit inside you to grow?
Was it serving others that nurtured kindness so?
For your life was like a well-tended garden
Filled with His kindness, sweetness, and pardon.
Your sandal prints lead us into His kindly pace;
Thank you, dear sister, for walking in His grace.

16

Tender

♥♡♥

*"How often I wanted to gather your children together, the
way a hen gathers her chicks under her wings."*
(MATTHEW 23:37)

Synonyms: warm, pitying, merciful

*M*y mom's small stature contrasts with her enormous
heart. I've often wondered how the Lord fit a 6' heart into a 4'-
10"-inch frame. Mom is a mix of lion and lamb, of mighty and
mild, and of tough and tender. I watched her stand her ground
at a large hospital when the personnel tried to force her to go
home at night and leave my dying father. Not only did this lion
not leave that night, but she also sat at his bedside for four
weeks until he took his last agonized breath. Ever so tenderly,
this lamb comforted him in every way she could and reassured
him by her faithful vigil until his passing.

Mom also tended to my Mamaw (grandmother) as long as
she could after Mamaw, at the age of 96, fell and broke her hip.
When my mom's finances no longer allowed her to keep
Mamaw at home, Mom then kept close vigil at the convalescent
home until Mamaw's death.

These accounts are typical of my mom's tenderhearted
ways. She cares about people and has a way of expressing that
ever so gently with her availability and tender touch.

Mom now has Alzheimer's, yet still the sweetness of the Lord's Spirit rests on her. I've watched, as I introduce her to others, how folks are drawn to her warm, endearing ways.

Recently we were together, and Mom drifted in and out of remembering who I was. But even when she didn't know me, she would lean over, pat my arm, and tell me I seemed like a really nice person. I replied, "That's because you raised me." She responded sweetly, "I'm so glad I did."

Tenderness is definitely a quality indicative of someone who has had hardships or has been broken and has allowed the Lord to use her deep ache to eventually—and discreetly—help others. My new friend Andrea, who just moved into my neighborhood, is an example.

Andrea is a vibrant, lovely young lady with long, dark hair and a smile that warms your heart. In her living room is a photograph of her tall, handsome husband holding their darling baby girl, named Angie. They appear to be a picture-perfect family. And they are in a loving way, for they care deeply for each other. But they have a long road ahead of them. You see, shortly after marrying her sweetheart, Andrea found out her husband had a brain tumor. The surgeries that followed left him functioning at a child's level. So now Andrea, instead of being his wife, has become his caretaker and mother figure. How life-altering for all three of them.

When I found out about Andrea's situation, I was impressed with the warmth that emanated from her and her tenderhearted responses to others in pain. She takes time out from her caretaking duties periodically to meet with other cancer patients and their family members, to comfort them and to assure them of God's ongoing provisions. That's just how Andrea sees life.

I wonder if Naomi at some point didn't stand back and observe the dearness of Ruth and thank the Lord for this tenderhearted daughter-in-law who had poured out kindness to Naomi in every possible way.

Others certainly took note. After Ruth married Boaz, she miraculously conceived (she previously had been unable to bear children) and gave birth. Then the town's women went to Naomi to celebrate her good fortune. They told her, "Your daughter-in-law, who loves you and is better to you than seven sons, has given birth to him [baby Obed]" (Ruth 4:15).

Better than seven sons?! That's a powerful statement since at that time boys were considered a greater blessing of the Lord than girls were. And the number seven represents completion and perfection. So it sounds as if they were saying to Naomi that Ruth was even better than if Naomi had had a houseful of perfect men.

Women like Ruth, Andrea, and my mom demonstrate for us that losses don't have to rob us of a quality life. They can, in fact, create in us the capacity for tenderness. If only we can learn to see it that way.

My mom said she was glad she raised me. Well, so am I, Mom. So am I.

17

Compassionate

♥♡♥

"She [Pharaoh's daughter] opened [the basket] and saw the baby. He was crying, and she felt sorry for him."
(EXODUS 2:6, NIV)

Synonyms: humane, unselfish, soft-hearted

*M*y friend Florence used to teasingly say she didn't have the gift of nurse-ness. I laughed heartily because I knew what she was saying. I was pretty understanding for the first day or two when my family members were ill. But by the third day, I wanted them to pick up their beds and walk. That was pretty nervy, because when the tables were turned—or should I say the bed covers, with me under them—I wanted everyone around me to be compassionate and long-suffering.

My, my, aren't we walking, talking dichotomies? We appreciate compassionate people, especially when they show up in the middle of our crisis. But don't ask us to deliberately walk in the direction of compassion, because to do so is to walk through the valley of the shadow of death. Or so it would seem to me.

Case in point: Mother Teresa. We all held her in high regard and had tremendous respect for her compassionate work, but who among us would leave the comfort of our La-Z-Boy to enlist in the good Mother's services? Who among us is willing—day in, day out, without applause or benefit—to tend to the earthy affairs of humankind? Who among us would willingly subject ourselves to disease and poverty?

For me, poverty is having to roll my own luggage to my hotel room because the bellhop is busy. I'm not proud of that; that's a confession. As far as disease is concerned, I carry hand sanitizer almost everywhere I go, lest a germ dare linger on my finger. And I have felt close to hostile toward folks in the grocery line who sneeze and wheeze in my direction. So how do you think I'd do tending running sores?

I'm grateful we aren't all called to be Mother Teresa—or are we? Certainly we aren't all directed to move to Calcutta, but we are all called to see others' pain and to care about and for others in compassionate ways. We can all speak kindly to our mothers-in-law, go where God sends us with grateful hearts, and accept even humble jobs graciously . . . like Ruth.

Ruth offered to glean in the barley and wheat fields to provide for Naomi and herself. Even the word *glean* (ugh, notice the word *lean* in it) causes my dry bones to lock up. Then add to *glean* the word *field*, as in vast, as in endless rows, as in scorching earth, as in somebody grab the sunscreen—please! Ruth saw an opportunity to be compassionate toward her mother-in-law; I see only the hard work it takes to express that compassion. I could use a vision check.

As a matter of fact, I received one as a teenager, when I picked potatoes with rows of other pickers in an attempt to make some quick, easy change. Quick, easy? Huh! It was backbreaking, dirty, hot, and exceedingly boring. I lasted an hour before I began to whine. Suddenly helping out by peeling potatoes in my mom's kitchen didn't seem like such cruel and unusual punishment.

But I must say, potato picking does put one in the right position to learn about compassion—on one's knees. I should have stayed there longer . . . much longer. Mother Teresa's life included daily prayer times in which she invited the Compassionate One to live more fully through her.

I wonder what would happen if, say, three times a day, we simply asked the Lord to work compassion into our hearts? Perhaps we would be more charitable even with our in-laws, follow where He leads even if it's to a stable in Bethlehem, and

serve others even if we have to lean or kneel or practice nurse-ness. Hmm, I just wonder.

Perhaps you noted along Ruth's road that her qualities— compassion, kindness, softness, sensitivity, and tenderness— though different, are intercon- nected. Compassion is extended by kind people who are soft in their man- ner, sensitive in their respon- siveness, and tender toward others. I believe this lovely package of qualities is representative of the muted shades of womanhood. This capacity allows us the opportunity to touch our world with the delicacies of our femininity. Thank You, Lord, for our genteel-faceted design.

18

A Place of Grace:
A Prayer

❤♡❤

*W*hat would you have us see, Lord, in Ruth's journey? That her gaze was steady and her ways were kind? That she saw more than she said, and when she spoke, her words were thought out and compassionate? Perhaps the tenderhearted way in which she embraced her relative is what You didn't want us to miss.

For each of us You may want to illuminate something different, something that fits our struggle, our need, our family, our failure, our faith. We want Your best, and we see in Ruth's life how You sovereignly turned devastation around, like traveling another bend in the road, until You brought her to a new place abounding with Your grace.

We long for Your fruitful ways that our lives might be so laden with Your bounty You find us bent low in praise. Lead us through our valleys, down the dusty roads of change, through our loneliness, and bring us to Your fields full of promise.

We saw Sister Ruth cling, serve, walk, kneel, work, and lie

down. Now, may we be willing to do the same. May we cling to You, serve others willingly, walk in Your ways, kneel in Your presence, work while it's day, and lie down in quietness and peace. Amen.

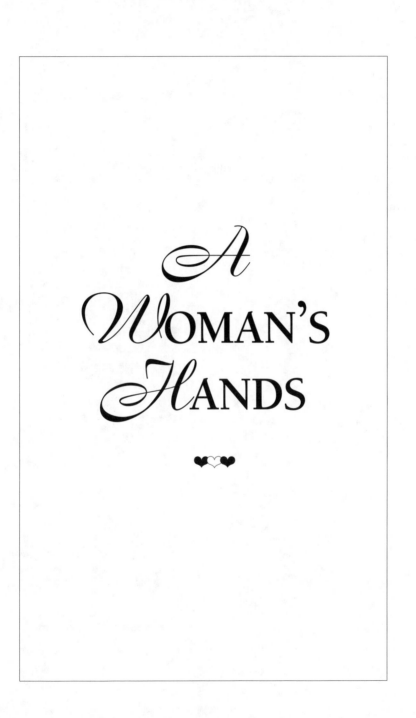

A WOMAN'S HANDS

19

Mrs. Perfection Meets Ms. Im-: The Proverbs 31 Woman

❤♡❤

*D*oes the Proverbs 31 woman have a name? I vote for "Mrs. Gets on Your Nerves" or "Mrs. I Have No Friends Because I'm So Perfect." I know, I know. I shouldn't think like that, but she is so squeaky clean it makes me want to oil her. Surely her joints must be stiff by now from holding everything together over the centuries. This gal needs a trip to a spa, a masseuse, or at least the local Jiffy Lube.

P-31 sounds like the wishful conjugating of a mother who wanted only the best of a woman's qualities for her son. Bible scholars suggest that King Lemuel was Bathsheba's name for Solomon. You know, a nickname like Lambie Pie or Dumpling. But the name Lemuel had deeper meaning ("belonging to God"). King Lemuel tells us in Proverbs 31 what his mama told him about the kind of cloth an excellent wife is cut from. It's a heavenly fabric such as none of us has ever donned.

To be kind, I have to admit verses 10 through 31 list a number of worthy goals and a set of excellent standards for women. I know I need examples. In fact, some years ago (23 to be exact), I pleaded with the Lord to bring a woman into my life who would be a mentor, an example to me. His answer at that time was "I'm not going to give you an example; I want you to become one."

Don't think that didn't set my disorganized, unstable heart to palpitating wildly. I was more than willing to observe another woman living out truth, but to rise to the call of doing it myself—well, that was a mop of a different color. Believe me, a mop was the least of what it would take to clean up my act. I'm grateful that along the way the Lord eventually did send women who were excellent examples for me to learn from. But He has also required me to continue to grow up.

In reality I already had examples in my life, but I hadn't seen them for what they were. Perhaps you do, too. For me, it took time, healing, maturing, and personal experience before I realized what an example my mom had been. That insight came to me after I had stumbled over my fair share of personal failures that tenderized my heart and made me more merciful regarding others' failures.

You see, my mom didn't do everything right, but once I forgave her for not being perfect, I realized she did far more right than wrong. I encourage women today that, if they have issues with their moms, they resolve them as quickly as possible so they can enjoy their mothers and appreciate them. Before we know it, time flits by and our mothers are no longer with us.

My mom might not have been perfect like Mrs. P-31, but she sure was handy with her hands. She could organize, customize, and economize. She could take a shack and transform it into a cottage. She could take a chicken and concoct a feast. And she could take a nickel and create a bankroll. I don't know how she did what she did with what she had, but perhaps growing up in a large family on a farm, living through the Depression, and marrying a milkman gave her opportunity to be creative, versatile, resourceful, and industrious. Just like you-know-who, "Mrs. Got It All Together P-31."

Occasionally, I meet women who appear to have it all together, but on closer inspection (the old white-glove test), seldom is that true. I can say across the board that the people I've met are just that—people. They sometimes waste time, break the bank, burn the bacon, spew anger, and lose their way.

But that's what is so wearing about Mrs. P-31; no weaknesses are noted. This I know: If she does exist, I don't want to live beside her. I beat myself up enough already, thank you. You see, some days I leave lipstick in my jacket pocket and then launder the jacket, glazing my washing machine and dryer in Mambo Mauve. Other days I mail our taxes without the check in the envelope. The government, which has no humor, frowns on this. And then I scorch supper beyond recognition. (Actually, we aren't always sure what it is *before* I burn it.) So I'm not yet a P-31, or even a B-52 because I can hardly get off the ground to get my day going.

I console myself that I've made progress, and, dear sisters, if I understand this journey correctly, measurable, loving progress is what it's all about. P-31, in all her perfection, is an ideal to strive toward. We won't reach her heights, but we're bound to be better just for trying, as long as we don't become tied to the earth by legalistically attempting to be perfect.

Proverbs 31 highlights wonderful ways a woman can effectively and even eternally reach out to others. Six times in this famous passage, hands are mentioned, and many more times they are implied, suggesting the incredible influence of a woman's touch.

I find I must first reach up before I can effectively reach out. So take my hand and let's call on Him together. With His help, we can change our world even if we are less than perfect.

20

Creative

❤♡❤

"She makes linen garments and sells them."
(PROVERBS 31:24)

Synonyms: productive, original, imaginative

*E*vidently P-31 was quite the seamstress. Repeated references are made not only to her designing clothes for her family and for the marketplace, but also to her enjoyment of the activity. She was creative and happy to be so. Proverbs 31:13 says she worked with her hands in delight.

Now I, too, work with my hands in delight, but you can bet your loose buttons you won't find me zipping along on my Singer. Actually, the only stitching machine I own is my Mamaw's treadle, and I'm not certain where it is. Possibly it's encased in silken spider threads in the storage shed. No, a seamstress I'm not. I'm more into Velcro affixing, staple gunning, and push pinning (that last one's a tad uncomfortable as a hemline, though).

My hands-on work is more in the arenas of decorating, gardening, and Scrabble (that's work?). Although I have been known to hand off responsibility, hand down clothing, hand over loans (minuscule), and hand out advice.

When you think about it, hands are a wonderful part of our

anatomy. We can applaud others; hold someone else's hand; embrace our mom, sweetheart, or baby; extend our hands in friendship; wave; beckon; make music; and even whistle louder with them. The possibilities are endless.

Hands are lovely, even old hands. I loved tracing my grandmother's periwinkle veins as they ribboned around under her paper-thin skin. Thanie died at 97 years old, and her hands had given and received much throughout her lifetime. I remember watching her in my childhood as she smoothed the pages of her Bible, to which she turned in her search for added wisdom. And with fondness I recollect her hands preparing oatmeal and toast with dollops of her homemade peach preserves, which she served to me, her eager, drooling granddaughter.

I love babies' hands with their chubby little digits. Their fingers reach to grasp rattles, hanks of hair, and earrings as they dangle precariously from one's elongated earlobes. Their hands trust ours to steady them as we guide them into their first solo steps. Eventually we teach them to grasp a bat, toss a ball, and tie a bow. And before long, they teach us a few things, like handing over our car keys and cash. (I believe this is when we begin pulling out our own hair.) And they call this the circle of life?

A sweet memory for me is my mom ironing. She could have taught lessons on it at the university because her ironing was a work of art. She even refrigerated it. She would fill a basin with a starch solution, soak doilies, roll them, refrigerate them, and then iron them into submission. She would fool with the ruffles until each one stood in peaked perfection. And you should have seen her press curtains, draperies, and bedspreads until they were pleated or mashed just as she wanted them. Yes, Mom worked with her hands in delight—both hers and ours.

My son Jason brags that he received an A in ironing in high school. Now, I've never actually seen any of his handiwork, but I know he doesn't refrigerate it. At least I've never seen any of it parked between the peanut butter and the hot dogs in our fridge. His wife, Danya, assures me she hasn't noticed him, in their three years of marriage, huddled over an ironing board either, or even walking near one. But he's a good son and a fine husband, and Danya and I give him an A also . . . for handing out far-fetched lines that keep us giggling.

Giggling is what filled our home years ago when I inadvertently stitched my husband's pants leg together. He couldn't deny that I had mastered a severe stitch, restricting any hope of entry.

Speaking of entry, I remember the entrance of one Jason Robert Clairmont into our lives on April 22, 1974. This momentous occasion called for a few stitches, too, if my memory serves me well. His daddy was so pleased, he almost popped his buttons, but he knew I couldn't sew them back on. The doctor handed us our son, who touched our hearts and changed our lives.

I love being a woman, and I'm grateful for the privilege of being a mom as well. I may not sew so well, but I have mended my share of broken toys. I don't iron like my mom, but I have offered a hand during pressing times. And I've learned through the years and the tears the importance of smoothing out the wrinkles in my life with wisdom from the Scriptures . . . even Proverbs 31.

21

Versatile

❤🤍❤

"She looks well to the ways of her household."
(PROVERBS 31:27)

Synonyms: multifaceted, handy, adaptable

*M*y dad used to tell me when I was a youngster not to put his hat on lest I lose my hair the way he did. But somehow I just couldn't resist donning his cap when he wasn't looking. I'm grateful Dad wasn't prophetic, because 45 years later I'm still sporting a massive wad of unruly hair.

Today I continue to wear hats, not my dad's but a ton of my own. They're not the kind you buy from a milliner (are there still such people?), but the imaginary ones that represent real roles in our lives. For instance, I have a writer's cap, similar to a thinking cap (whatever that is). And even though you can't see the hat, you can see the reality of my efforts in books.

I also don a chef's hat from time to time. It doesn't happen very often or for very long, but occasionally my culinary cleverness needs to be released. Of course, that's my opinion. Those who have shared in my gourmet goodies may have thought I should have capped my epicurean urges. (Truth be known, my hat would have been more succulent than my ham.)

My wife's hat is a doozie. It's a cross between a fez and a

beanie . . . with pockets. The pockets hold things my hubby laid down that I, P-31 woman that I am, pick up—important things like the remote control, the nail clippers, the phone, the Super Glue, and the car registration. I considered Super Gluing the remote to his forehead to save us time and frustration, but his hat got in the way. Curiously, his turban has pockets, too. Uh-oh. They hold my car keys, my wallet, my pantyhose, my charge card, and other assorted debris that I misplaced. Hmm, maybe we should just exchange headgear.

Actually, I have more hats than sense; or to say it another way, some of my hats are senseless. By wearing too many, one can easily overextend one's, uh, sombrero, which can really trip us up. I, for one, have stumbled while trying to exchange one basket of hat tricks for another.

We already know P-31 didn't indulge in idleness. And we know that to specialize in siestas is to miss the joys of a woman's extensive capabilities. So, pray tell, how does a woman maintain her sanity while functioning in her versatility?

Well, take note of our Proverbs friend, who certainly was a busy babe (different from a busybody) and filled many roles. She was attentive to her family's needs, she was a business-woman, she was a seamstress, she was a charity worker, and she was a teacher. Go, girl, go.

Unfortunately, Scripture doesn't tell us how she balanced her obligations and managed to maintain a caring touch. I know I tend to get heavy-handed when I'm dashing breathlessly from one role to another. Perhaps that's the key. When we are unable to do what is before us with gentleness and kindness, we have lost sight of our calling and are sporting more hats than heart.

Who cares that at the end of a day we've achieved tons more than our next-door neighbor if we are like Attila the Hun in the process? I've seen charitable acts done by folks who

Guideposts.

Don't miss an issue of inspiration! Order your own subscription or delight a friend with a gift subscription.

Preferred Subscriber Guarantee

1. We guarantee that you may cancel your subscription(s) at any time upon request and that you will receive a prompt refund on any unserved issues.

2. We guarantee to continue your gift subscription(s) at the then current rate for as long as you wish, without interruption, unless you instruct us to stop.

3. We guarantee if you include your own subscription we will also provide continuous service at the then current rate for as long as you wish.

4. Send no money now. As a Preferred Subscriber, a gift card will be automatically sent in your name every year (on receipt of payment) to the person named on the reverse side.

(Please detach at perforation and mail card below.)

Guideposts
Subscription Order

guideposts.com\ins

Mail this card to start or renew your own subscription, give a friend a gift—*or do both.* And we'll surprise you with something special!

Send No Money — We'll Bill You Later

(Please detach at perforation and mail card below.)

☐ **1 YEAR $15.97** plus $.97 delivery
$19.94 Canadian/$28.94 Foreign (12 issues)

☐ **2 YEARS $23.97** plus $1.97 delivery
$31.94 Canadian/$49.94 Foreign (24 issues)

YOUR NAME: (Please print)

Address _____ Apt. _____

City _____ State _____ ZIP _____

E-mail _____

Include my own subscription for: ☐ Regular ☐ Large Print* (add $2.00 to the **above prices**)

Send a gift and a gift card in my name for: ☐ **1 Year** ☐ **2 Years**

GIFT TO: (Please print)

Address _____ Apt. _____

City _____ State _____ ZIP _____

☐ Regular ☐ Large Print* (add $2.00 to the above prices)

J1051IDA

*Intended for the visually impaired.

guideposts.c

should have stayed home and rested until they could be civil (me included). The Proverbs approach shows P-31 extending her versatility (wife, mom, leader, entrepreneur) and offering a helping hand with kindness on her tongue and a smile on her face.

I don't think it's possible to speak kindly and have a bright countenance unless we are tending to our own needs: spending time in His presence, spending time in prayer, spending time in laughter, and even spending some time in tears. It will take that to keep us sane, sweet, sincere, and smiling.

We women are amazing! We achieve so much, often in short time frames, such as our children's last-minute homework projects due in the morning. Or tossing together a spur-of-the-moment dinner and stretching the soup to feed drop-in guests. Not to mention developing a snazzy wardrobe on a shoestring budget while creating a home environment that welcomes and comforts.

And that's just the beginning of our opportunities to change and influence our world. May we do these things and more, not in a prideful way, but wearing the protective covering (hat) of humility.

Proverbs 31 tells us our friend handmade coverings for herself. I wonder what her headwear looked like? I can picture her as she arranged it in soft folds draped around her face. And I would imagine that, as lovely as it was, it didn't compare to the beauty of her heart and hand outstretched toward others.

22

Resourceful

❤♡❤

"She selects wool and flax and works with eager hands."
(PROVERBS 31:13, NIV)

Synonyms: ingenious, inventive, enterprising

I was consistently amazed, when I was growing up, at what my mom could concoct out of leftovers, spare parts, damaged goods, and meager findings. She looked "well to the ways of her household" (verse 27), just like the P-31 woman. Whether my mom used her hands to transform what was left in the pantry at the end of the month to look like a banquet, or she created a whole new look in the house with the same old stuff, she truly was resourceful. Today I appreciate that far more than I did when I was a child. Oh, I enjoyed the benefits of her resourcefulness even then, but now I also admire her attitude and her ingenuity.

You might wonder what attitude has to do with being resourceful. Well, plenty. I believe resourceful folks are positive individuals who are always looking for ways to make things work, especially when something goes wrong, when an item falls short, or when the funds dry up. Instead of giving up or giving in, they rise to the occasion. In fact, the word *resource* comes from a French word that means "to rise again."

I believe any time your mind is open, you think more expansively. Rather than whining, "This isn't going to fly," you instead inquire, "How else might I do this?" That positive approach starts the creative juices flowing and has been the birthing room for many inventions. When we don't see a failed attempt as a dead-end road, and when we don't internalize the difficulty as something "that always happens (only) to me," then we often can move beyond the snag in the fabric of our lives to find an imaginative tapestry.

Speaking of stitches (we were, weren't we?), my mom would use her hands to take balls of thread and transform them into exquisite, floor-length tablecloths. She wouldn't sell them, but instead regularly bequeathed them to thrilled recipients. Crocheting was my mom's way of being resourceful during her rocking-chair era. A ball of thread for me would be like a formless and void mass, and if left to crochet with it, I would produce a formless and void mess. I would not excel at thread resourcing whether I was in a rocking chair or a rocket ship.

Once I threaded hundreds of hand-cut snowflakes, which were hung from the heavens (actually a meeting-room ceiling) to create snow flurries for a holiday party. And one year my friend Edith and I stitched a truckload of ties for our husbands. Well, actually Edith ended up repairing most of mine because they looked more like Hawaiian bibs than suit ties. Okay, so I'm a little loosely stitched together, and my thread is a bit bare, but I'm resourceful and my attitude is good . . . uh, most of the time.

We can see P-31 was resourceful with her hands (verses 13, 19, 20, 22, 24), her time (verses 15, 18, 27), and her finances (verses 16, 18, 24, 25, 27). And she displayed a sterling attitude as she thought of others, pursued her tasks with vigor, and faced her life with confidence and poise.

P-31 has always gotten on my nerves with her perfectionistic ways, but the more time I spend with her . . . well, the more

I like her and the less threatening she is. I guess anytime I find someone who excels in so many areas I feel a tad insecure. I measure my worth next to her accomplishments, and my value plummets. I guess that's why the Lord has His own measuring stick for us, why He gave us different gifts, and why He made us all capable of being resourceful. He wants us to be resourceful, to "rise again" in every circumstance of our lives and with His help to do the best we can with what we have.

I love that we can be women whose main resource is Jesus. And I love that He allows us to use our hands in skillful ways. Just as He used His hands as a carpenter to create, we can, with our touch, help shape our world into a better place. That causes my heart to celebrate and my hands to clap!

I never cease to be amazed at how resourceful Jesus is. He not only rose again, but He also agreed to take our leftovers, our spare parts, our damaged goods, and our meagerness and use them all in our best interest and for His glory.

23

Industrious

❤❤❤

*"She considers a field and buys it; from her
earnings she plants a vineyard."*
(PROVERBS 31:16)

Synonyms: diligent, busy, skillful

Industrious speaks of activity. I'm active. *Industrious* speaks of productivity. I produce. *Industrious* speaks of follow-through and unwavering steadiness. I'm active.

Industrious sounds like such a sturdy word, and I often feel—you guessed it—unsturdy. Actually, at times I feel overwhelmed by life, especially the little details, such as maintaining a semblance of order in my surroundings so crowbars aren't needed to open and close my dresser drawers. And so I don't humiliate myself when I open my purse in public, and it looks like a garage sale in progress. And so an unexpected visitor doesn't find my desk encased with towers of printed matter, which leaves me a babbling imbecile.

Somehow stuff accumulates not only in my closets, drawers, purses, basement, glove compartment, and desk, but it also weighs heavily on my emotions. Disorder discombobulates me. Now I'm aware an industrious, hands-on approach enables me to corral my personal debris, tame it, and maintain it.

I would love to have peeked into P-31's chariot to see if she ever stuffed emergency pantyhose in her glove compartment. Nah, probably not. But surely at times family litter, pantry pile-ups, and castle clutter challenged her. Yet Scripture tells us her family rose up to bless her.

I've been in homes where, if the family did rise up, it wouldn't be able to find Mom over the mounds of unfolded laundry, craft projects, and discarded reading materials, much less see her to bless her. Oh my. That was me last Wednesday.

I guess that's why Proverbs instructs us to study the ants (6:6-8 and 30:25) to see a demonstration of industriousness. Those little creatures Reebok throughout their day with seldom even a coffee break. They seem to know their purpose, and they are determined to get their job done one bite at a time. No matter how many obstacles are placed in their path, they are not deterred.

As a matter of fact, we had a legion of ants move into a tree trunk in our front yard. Those industrious little twerps proceeded to eat out the inside of a 50-foot maple. By the time we realized that our maple had become their McDonald's, they had weakened the interior structurally until our house was under threat of the tree toppling onto our bedroom—on my side of the bed.

Now, if teeny-tiny ants can pull off toppling a tree a gazillion times larger than themselves, what are we capable of accomplishing? Actually, many women have industriously used their time, talent, and determination to do the impossible: women like Florence Nightingale, who used her hands to reduce drastically the death rate not only in a war but also in hospitals throughout the world. Florence worked unflaggingly, training her own nurses in proper sanitation to protect them and to ensure the well-being of their patients.

Dorothea Dix was asked to teach a Sunday school class at a

house of correction in 1841 and was shocked to observe the horrific treatment of the insane and mentally ill who were incarcerated with criminals, regardless of age and sex. The mentally ill were left unclothed, in darkness, without heat or sanitary provisions. Some were chained and beaten. Dorothea worked for the next 40 years, inspiring legislators in 15 states and Canada to establish state hospitals for the mentally disturbed. Her hands-on follow-through was rewarded when 32 institutions in the United States were built because of her dogged efforts.

Louisa May Alcott volunteered her services as a nurse following the Civil War. As a result, she contracted typhoid and never fully recovered. Even in her frailty, she began to write, and in 1868 and 1869 she penned her most famous work, *Little Women*. She lived to be 56 and spent her last years using her compassionate hands to care for her sickly parents until their deaths. Louisa died two days after her father, leaving behind a treasure trove of beloved books.

And I become mired because my desktop needs tending, or my purse needs to be dumped and slimmed down? I guess I bought into the slogan "I deserve a break today." It really isn't that I can't take care of the accumulation in my life; it's that I find that kind of work drudgery. I wonder how I would have done with the laborious, thankless task of fighting for the mentally ill. Or how I would have handled the filth and unsanitary conditions in hospitals while trying to inspire change. Or how I would have cared for others when I desperately needed someone to care for me.

I don't know about you, but I think I'll join P-31 and use my hands to tidy up my own life and then reach out to others with greater fervor and dedication. Maybe I can't attain the legacy of a Florence Nightingale, but I can—one tiny bite at a time—begin to learn what it means to be a truly industrious woman in my sphere of influence. I want to be one who tackles whatever needs to be done and then sees it through to completion. Timber!

Now, has anyone seen my purse?

24

Hands to the Task: A Prayer

❤♡❤

$\mathcal{L}$ ord, You knew all along how important and how deeply satisfying it would be for a woman to use her hands to touch other's lives, whether that be crocheting a tablecloth or cleansing a wound. You created us with hands that we might work, mend, design, adorn, embrace, serve, cuddle, assure, lift, pray, and praise. The possibilities for our outreach appear endless. How thrilling for us.

But sometimes there is more to do than time allows. Prioritize our efforts as You direct our steps. We don't want to spread our offerings so thin that no one benefits. We want our touch to heal, to soothe, to unite, and to restore.

When others look at the fruit of our labor, may it be sweet, appealing, and beneficial. We want to reach out in loving ways like our Proverbs 31 example, who put hands to her faith and enriched all whom she touched.

Sometimes that which needs to be done is so unappealing. Help us to be dedicated to the work at hand regardless of how distasteful it might be. For we are confident that, if You gave it to us to tend to, You have purposes beyond what we see. May no task be too menial or too mammoth for us to put our hand to it with faithful determination. If You find us hesitant, may we be reminded of Your hands, Your nail-pierced hands that reached out to us. Amen.

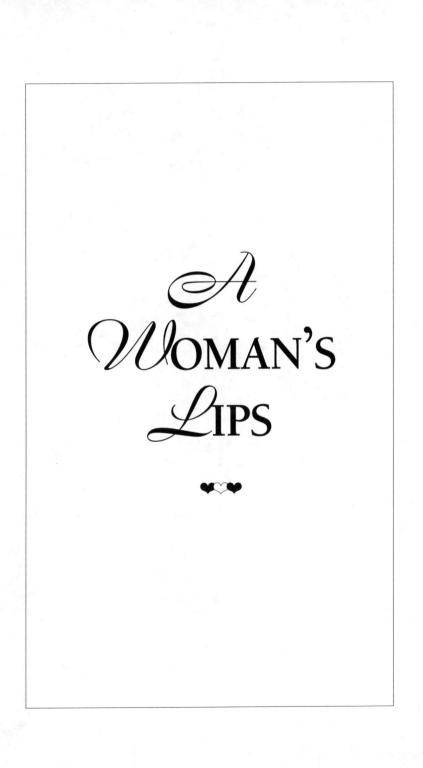

A
Woman's
Lips

25

Humility in High Places: Esther

❤♡❤

I think every little girl dreams of being a princess and maybe a queen, but soon life dispels those fairy-tale thoughts. By junior high school, we realize the most one might hope for is the minuscule possibility of being named homecoming queen. But that reign is short-lived and comes with little opportunity to exercise the power of one's throne.

I mean, if I make queen, I want to be known as queen and shown as queen, but I also want to rule. Yes! Ask my children; this queen loves to rule. That is, until I'm too tired or circumstances become too complicated or too intense. Then I want to pass my crown on to another.

Speaking of passing on, Queen Vashti gave up her reign and crown when she refused to respond to King Ahasuerus's command (the king has spoken!) to come to the palace and parade before the people and the princes. Technically, she didn't really pass on the crown; she was actually stripped of it, which, by the way, was how she was asked to present herself in public—stripped. Or so it is suggested. Apparently, in the king's inebriated condition, he decided he wanted the people and visiting rulers to see all of Vashti's beauty. When the queen refused to appear, the command was given, "Off with her crown!"

First, may I say, "Hurrah for Vashti!" She knew that to refuse the king (just say no) was to put her life and her crown in jeopardy. She also knew his request was unwise, unhealthy, and violated her personage. Even if his request had been for the queen to prance clothed in front of a drunken crowd so that others might leer at her beauty, the command would have been degrading. She made the choice that was right for her, and while it cost her the throne, it didn't cost her personal dignity. (Ladies, take notes.)

Eventually, the king longed for a new queen to fill the vacancy, and a lengthy beauty pageant began. The qualifications were simple: The queen must be young, beautiful, and a virgin (what a surprise). Among the "contestants" was Esther, a lovely Jewish woman who lived with her Uncle Mordecai following her parents' deaths. Under Uncle Mordie's counsel, Esther didn't make known who her people were to anyone at the palace.

As one of the finalists in the beauty pageant, she was housed in the harem to prepare to meet the king. Get this, gals. She was given seven maids to tend to her every need and treated to one year—that's 52 weeks; I mean we're talking 365 days—of spa living. (Twenty minutes in a tub and I'm a raisin. Guess I'm disqualified right there.)

History tells us that his majesty flipped his royal crown (not cola) when he saw Esther, and in time he made her his queen. But her highness Esther soon found herself in a thickening, if not sickening, plot. Seems Haman, a high-ranking officer, hated Mordecai and decided to rid the region of Jews. But Haman didn't realize Mordecai was the queen's uncle or that her highness was a Jew. Hmm, this sounds like a soap opera.

Haman managed to have an irreversible edict passed that all Jews (women and children included) must be destroyed—as in killed, as in annihilated. Imagine all that hostility in one heart, all because Mordecai refused to bow down in Haman's presence.

Oh, the haughty, self-absorbed heart of humankind that would require others to pay homage to a person: Look at me, acknowledge me, honor me, life's all about me. That type of demand always leads to demise.

Mordecai sent a message to his niece, Esther, that she must go before the king and plead their people's case. Esther's first response appeared to be fearful intimidation, for no one was allowed to enter the king's presence without his invitation. However, if you showed up invitationless, he could extend his golden scepter when he saw you approach, granting you safe access to his throne.

The king hadn't sent Esther an invitation for a month. So, when she risked approaching him, I'm sure her knees were clattering under her royal petticoats.

His highness received her, and when he asked what her pleasure was, she invited him to dinner. Dinner? Excuse me, but people were going to die, and she wanted to dine? If I had been her, and he had asked me what I wanted, I'm sure I would have blurted out every bit of my request, leaving nothing unsaid. Instead, Esther sealed her lips and carefully, prayerfully waited on God's timing. And when it was time for Esther to speak up, everything fell into place, including Haman's body, as he dangled from the gallows on which he had planned to hang Mordecai.

Esther makes me proud to be a woman. She was wise enough to wait and then brave enough to speak up. That's a difficult balance. Esther's lips spoke the truth in a timely way. Oh, the power of well-placed words.

As a child, when I imagined myself as a member of royalty,

I didn't consider the costs, only the benefits. I wanted to bellow orders, not kneel before the king. I wanted to soak in the spa, not walk a thin line. I desired a life of fame and ease, not responsibility and humility. Hmm, I wonder if that's why we are instructed "to do away with childish things"? When I behave as a child, I speak as though life is all about me, and that opens my heart up to receive seeds of offense, bitterness, and hostility. Then I become a high-minded Haman instead of a humble Esther.

Do I want to hang or reign? That's not a difficult decision, but the journey can be. The high cost of being regal and maintaining personal dignity means the path to the palace is sometimes perilous, the throne will have contenders, and the crown has, at times, thorns.

26

Expressive

❤♡❤

"A time to be silent and a time to speak."
(ECCLESIASTES 3:7).

Synonyms: eloquent, informative, pithy

*T*hose of you well acquainted with Esther might wonder why I chose the hesitant queen as an example of expressiveness instead of, say, New Testament Martha. Now, she had plenty to say, especially when things weren't going her way. I identify with her being a tad . . . um, let's call it "effusive," which is why I appreciate a more reluctant yet heroic woman like Esther. She waited for the right moment and then emptied her arsenal of words. My tendency is to shoot a lot of blanks, saying things that should have been left either unsaid or spoken at a more suitable time. Esther was both wise in waiting and wise in words. That made her my choice for Wonder Woman of the Word Award.

No fooling. I'm impressed with anyone who demonstrates her maturity by measuring her words and dispensing them appropriately. I tend to be a bottom-line kind of gal, which can be refreshing or can blow others away because being forthright can startle, disarm, or offend the listener. Coming to understand how jarring truth can be has taught me to leave people a hiding place in case they need to take refuge from my vocal volleys. As liberating as truth can be, it also has the power to intimidate, frighten, and bring pain, which should never be our goal.

I used to believe, when I was the one doling out truth, that if a person couldn't deal with bare-bones honesty, that was her problem. Then, when the tables were turned and I was the one dodging someone else's bullets, scampering for cover, and feeling the nakedness of my own vulnerability, I began to reconsider my approach. I tell you, there's nothing like personal experience to change one's mind and heart.

Today I'm still in training as I learn the life skill of using words more discriminatingly. Sometimes my tendency still is to say something unkind because, shucks, my day isn't going well.

I snarled at my husband the other day when he asked me what my plans were for dinner. His question was appropriate and innocent, but I was taxed, my desk was erupting in mail, I was behind on a deadline, and what I heard was one more demand. Actually, he wanted to take me out to dinner, and he was checking to see if that would work for me. Of course, after my charming response, I'm surprised he didn't ask for separate tables.

Scripture warns us that out of the contents of the heart the mouth speaks, which should alert a number of us to our need for a heart specialist. He who created us is willing to examine, diagnose, operate, and heal our wounded, broken, and clogged hearts. The Lord is just waiting for us to sign the consent form.

Esther was asked to speak up at a time when it would have been easier to clam up. I love the queen's response to her threatening situation. She first fasted and prayed and then implored others to join her. So when she went before the king to ask that her people be spared from annihilation, she approached according to the Lord's directive and under the protective covering of prayer.

Her initial conversation with the king was brief and invitational. She didn't sound desperate or hysterical, but instead asked the king to join her for a private banquet prepared for him and Haman. The king obliged her, and that evening the two men dined to their satisfaction.

After dinner, the king offered Esther whatever she desired up to half the kingdom. That must have been some meal; I'd like to have that recipe. I mean, the king's offer would be the same as a wealthy husband handing his wife a new credit card and telling her to buy whatever made her happy.

Instead of making her request known, though, Esther invited the two men back the following evening for yet another meal. The next night, when the mealtime was over, she shared her concerns with the king. I love what happened next. The king sought Esther's counsel on how to resolve the issues to her satisfaction. That's when she spoke boldly and placed the bottom line clearly before the king. He received her words as wisdom and granted her requests.

Whew! The threat on an entire nation was averted because one woman knew when to be still and when to speak up, when to seal her lips and when to unseal them. And even more importantly, she knew to present herself to the King of the Universe before she made her way into the presence of King Ahasuerus.

And that, expressive and nonexpressive friends, is our greatest need: to present ourselves to King Jesus. He will help us understand when we need to be still, what needs to be spoken, and when it should be said. All the while, He is both examining our motives and transforming our hearts.

I love being an expressive woman, especially when I seek the Lord's counsel. For He alone can save me and others (like my hubby) from the volumes—and I do mean volumes—of ramblings and grumblings within me. And get this: I can enter

His courts without an invitation or waiting for a golden scepter to be extended. And our King always is available to dine with us.

Excuse me. I believe that's Him now . . . knocking at the door.

27

Exquisite

*"She speaks with wisdom, and faithful
instruction is on her tongue."*
(PROVERBS 31:26, NIV).

Synonyms: elegant, richly wrought, matchless, refined

*Y*oung, beautiful, and a queen—what an exquisite (that is, "choice" or "flawless") existence. But life is never as it appears from the outside looking in, is it? Alas, Esther found her royal role rocked by conflict. Haman had tricked the king into signing a law that would annihilate Esther and Mordecai's future—as well as that of all Jews—unless someone intervened. Yet, if Esther followed her uncle's advice and spoke to the king about this matter without his formal invitation, it could be the end of her queenly reign, if not her life. And if she didn't speak up, it could be the end of her relatives and her. What a choice: to die or . . . to die.

The king already had demonstrated his intolerant nature when, with one wave of his golden scepter, he had dismissed his former queen from her queenship forever. That, I'm sure, was fresh in Esther's mind when her uncle told her to plead their people's cause. The poor girl was left in a dither. She had obeyed her uncle implicitly since she was a child, but what he asked now put her life in immediate risk. No wonder she hesitated. No wonder she fasted and prayed. And, yet, no wonder she finally obeyed.

Several clues hint at the relationship Esther had with Uncle Mordie. Her parents had died, and Mordecai had taken her into his home to raise her. That he received her as his daughter says a great deal about him, for young women in those times were not valued as young men were.

When Esther was ushered into the king's harem to spend a year in beauty preparations, the good uncle positioned himself outside the harem so that he might hear regular reports on her well-being. Mordecai paced back and forth and waited for someone to come out and bring him word about his beloved ward. That sounds like a concerned daddy to me.

When Mordecai covered himself with ashes in grief over the king's edict, Esther felt anguish for her uncle. No doubt they had a strong, loving relationship. And no wonder she finally received Mordecai's counsel, for this man not only loved her and their people, but he also loved God.

Still, it took some emphatic words from her uncle to nudge her out of her hesitancy and onto her knees. Listen to Mordecai's exhortation to Esther:

> Do not imagine that you in the king's palace can escape any more than all the Jews. For if you remain silent at this time, relief and deliverance will arise for the Jews from another place and you and your father's house will perish. And who knows whether you have not attained royalty for such a time as this? (Esther 4:13-14)

What a jolting reminder to us all. God doesn't need us, but we desperately need Him. In a moment He could raise up someone else in our stead. And while God chooses to involve us in His divine plans, considering our constant resistance, doesn't it make you wonder why? I'm grateful God is merciful and long-suffering.

When Esther bent her knee in relinquishment and willingness, He gave her words to speak, exquisite (choice) words of wisdom that would profoundly affect her people and their future. And her willingness to wait for the appropriate time to speak shows she had exquisite (flawless) timing. She wasn't trying to usurp authority or badger others with her opinions. Instead, in due time, she offered godly counsel, and because of her lack of arrogance, others were able to hear her and receive it.

I once heard an employee scream like a banshee at a co-worker. Even though what she said was true, the way she presented it cost her the respect of others as well as her promotion. Graciousness wins out over insolence every time.

Just as in Esther's situation, today God gives us the opportunity to speak truth that will make a difference to those in our circle of influence. We have the chance to show our own exquisite sense of timing and care.

It's not easy as women, with our rich heritage of emotions, to remain steady and stay on course for the long haul. I know my mom thought for a number of years that her training had fallen on deaf ears. My brother, sister, and I all seemed to be marching to the beat of our own drummer. But one by one, the drummer's beats miraculously turned into a melodious song. What rose up in our hearts was understanding of the exquisite hymn "What a Friend We Have in Jesus," the song we had heard sung in our home through our mother's lips. One by one, we bent our knees to the King of kings.

Perhaps the Lord has asked you to speak specific words to someone, maybe even to deliver a strong message. It may be to someone you love or someone in a position of authority. Remember that both Mordecai and Esther, before they spoke or sent a message, prayed fervently. Once you have done that and you still know it is you who needs to deliver the message, then do so in the Lord's timing and in His love. For who knows, dear one? Perhaps you are there for such a time as this.

I once stayed in my friend Ginny's home when she was walking through some relational problems. After retiring for the evening, I felt the Lord had given me an important insight for Ginny, but I didn't want to intrude on her personal struggle. That night I dreamed about what the Lord had said, and the next morning I awoke with it pressing on my mind. I still felt hesitant to share because I didn't want to make my dear friend feel bad. So I knelt down and prayed for direction.

When I stood, I was certain I should broach the subject. No sooner did I greet Ginny than she brought up the topic. So I carefully said, "I feel as though I might have an insight to help you." Ginny burst into tears, and I quickly backpedaled. "Never mind, Ginny. We don't need to talk about this, honest."

Ginny wiped her eyes and said, "No, it's okay. This morning during my quiet time the Lord told me He was going to use you to help me. I'm not upset; I'm grateful and I want to hear."

Cautiously yet honestly, I told her what I had observed, and she received my insights watered by her tears. Because of her teachable heart, what potentially could have been devastating was exquisitely liberating. And to think I almost bailed out at the first sign of struggle. But because of Ginny's determination to grow, we were able to stay with the Lord's agenda, and it became a change point in Ginny's circumstance.

She and I often remind each other of that occasion, when I was a hesitant messenger and she was a tentative hearer. Yet, how faithful God was to us both.

I like to think that on that day He considered both of us exquisite—not perfect, but choice and flawless as seen through His loving eyes—for working so hard to overcome our deficiencies. What a Friend we have in Jesus, what an exquisite Friend.

28

Expensive

❤♡❤

"A word aptly spoken is like apples of gold in settings of silver."
(Proverbs 25:11, NIV)

Synonyms: dear, high-priced, sumptuous

*H*ave you ever thought of your words as expensive? That what you say can cost you plenty and, quite honestly, be pricey for others as well? For instance, one inappropriate or unappreciated statement has cost many people a raise, a promotion, or even their job. A misunderstood comment or a deliberate jab has cost people their relationships with friends, relatives, and even their mates. Need I mention statements that have caused rivalries, feuds, and outright wars?

Some folks have found the cost of the words *I do* far more expensive than they were prepared to dole out. Or how about the words *I'm sorry*? Oh my, that one invariably knocks dents in our pride, and you know how much repairs can run these days. Then there's *I quit!* Now that phrase can cut into one's income. No doubt about it; words can be expensive.

Here's our dilemma: Many of us are naturally expressive, and some of what we have to say is exquisite and should be uttered. Yet far more of our verbiage is spewed into our atmosphere than anyone needs to hear.

Perhaps if we had to purchase each word we said aloud, we would be more conservative. In fact, I bet that would tone down idle prattle, cruel gossip, vexing controversies, and profanity. It could even shorten the eternal sales pitch, parental lectures, and bosses' endless demands. Hey, I think I'm onto something. How does $20 a sentence and $10 per vowel sound to you? And anyone who is heard spewing more than 100 words in a 15-minute span would have to pay an utterance fee.

Hmm, on second thought, this idea may be a case of muzzling my own ox. I definitely like to talk. As a matter of fact, I have been known to jabber, and I am given, on occasion, to gusts of gab exceeding an El Niño rain blast. I've heard that women have a greater need to articulate than our male counterparts. (Actually, I had figured that out before I was aware of any studies.) And we tend to use more words than men to say the same thing. (This will come as no surprise to the men.)

My friend's husband told her that she speaks like an Amplified Bible. Where one word will do, she uses four. I don't know if he meant that as a compliment or just as an observation. But like my friend, I love words; she and I would constantly be overdrawn or bankrupt if there were a word cop policing our verbosity.

The precious gift of a woman's expressiveness can be a gracious gift or a scathing sentiment. I have found the more wordy one is, the more likely she is to slip out with the inappropriate, the unkind, and the unnecessary. So a cautious approach would seem a wise consideration, especially for verbally effusive women like me.

If we wanted to play the piano, we would expect to practice endless hours before starring at Carnegie. If we planned to perform a double Lutz and a flying camel at the Olympics, we would anticipate repeatedly picking ourselves up off the ice during years of endless practice. So we should not be surprised that, if those of us who are wordy are to become more selective, we will need to practice silence.

I read about an actor who once a week for 24 hours refrained from speaking. I was impressed. My only concern was, if I were quiet that long, my words might build up inside me until I exploded. I can see it now . . . my family checking in on my silent effort and finding only vowels scattered about the room.

I do think vocabulary fasts would be healthy and helpful. Yet I'm also aware that, like Esther, I need to present myself before the Lord in prayer if I am to become an eloquent woman: a woman who is willing to pay the price of refraining from entering into foolish speculations, senseless small talk, and belligerent bickering; a woman who knows how to present truth wrapped in kindness, making it easier for others to accept and

unwrap it; a woman who is committed to curtailing her myriad opinions, opting for the welfare of her family, her community, and her world.

Esther's elocution lessons are a graceful reminder that we should be quick to listen and slow to speak. May we lean into her castle window and observe and absorb Queen Esther's wisdom. It was obtained at great expense and continues to pay off today for all who will learn the lesson.

One of the nice things about us women being expensive—whether verbally or otherwise—is that we have been purchased at an extravagant price. Considering that the word *expensive* hints at an item being bought for more than it was worth, the price paid to redeem us seems all the more extravagant. Now that's worth shouting from the palace gates.

29

Utterly Available: A Prayer

❤♡❤

*L*ord, I am amazed and grateful that You desire to converse with us. And quite honestly, I'm not sure at times how You get a word in edgewise. Quiet our incessant need to fill the air with chitchat. Open our reluctant lips when we carry Your message.

Esther was cautious and yet courageous. She was still and yet outspoken. She was young and yet wise. And You used her as Your messenger to protect a nation. How do You desire to use us?

You have given us language so that we might express our feelings for You and others. May we be sensitive to the leading of Your Spirit so that we pace both our walk and our talk. Teach us to be fluent in Your love and selective in our words, that what emanates from our lips may inspire others to learn, to grow, and to celebrate their lives. Amen.

A WOMAN'S MIND

❤❤

30

Food for Thought: Deborah

♥♡♥

I would like a tree named after me . . . perhaps a tall, stately one. Nah, I'm too petite for that. I wouldn't want a nut-bearing tree brandishing my name, that's for sure. Such a choice would be way too obvious, what with my bonkers personality. A weeping willow wouldn't do either—too reminiscent of my tendency to whine. I can hear the remarks now: "Go see the whiner; she's under the willow weeping." No, I think not. I know. How about an apple tree? It's fruitful yet short and gnarly. I'm sort of like that. Sometimes I have colorful offerings to extend to others and sometimes, quite honestly, I'm all bark.

This tree stuff started after I learned that Old Testament Deborah had a palm tree named after her. In fact, she would sit under the Palm of Deborah, and people would line up to receive her advice. Have I ever mentioned that I love to give advice? It's so much easier than taking it. Maybe I could have a palm named for me: Patsy Palm. Hmm, not quite as snazzy-sounding as the Palm of Deborah, is it? Never mind.

Now, this Deborah was a judge and a prophetess in a difficult time for God's people. Seems the Israelites couldn't behave themselves, so the Lord had allowed their enemies to overtake them. The men had lost their confidence and therefore their calling. That's when the Lord raised up a woman to be the judge over Israel. Deborah proved to be a bright light during a dark, bleak period of history.

I love that Deborah had the interior moxie and mental strength to rise to the occasion. In a culture that often didn't recognize women as having intelligence, and certainly didn't approve of women in leadership, becoming a judge could have been a threatening choice at best. But as we walk with Deborah, we will see her resiliency, intuitiveness, intelligence, steadiness, and fruitfulness. She filled her position ably, employing her mental agility, her sensible judgment, and God's grace.

Deborah, like many of us, was a woman with myriad responsibilities, many of which required mental agility. She was a wife, prophetess, judge, warrior, writer, and singer. You go, girl! How she did all that is beyond me, but then some days I wonder the same about myself and my friends. It seems we are a frenetic generation, like bees flitting in all directions.

Herein lies our challenge—to respond to our God-given call, rising to the occasion while remaining sweet. And I don't mean syrupy sweet, but sweet-spirited. We see in hardworking Deborah's life that even after the rigors of battle, a song comes forth from her lips. A sweet song of praise. Not a "mares eat oats and does eat oats" song of sweetness. Instead, she sings of strength and victory.

Of all her roles, the one that surprises me most is that of the warrior. When the army's leader, Barak, was commanded by the Lord through Deborah's counsel to engage the enemy, Barak refused to go without Deborah. She agreed and stood with Barak until the enemy was defeated. The victory was miraculous, with the Lord providing a pelting rainstorm that caused the enemy's iron chariots to become mired in mud. While the men tried to free their wheels, Barak and his army swooped down from the mountains and ended their foe's tyrannical rule.

Imagine a woman serving as co-commander to ten thousand men who had to face a formidable, well-equipped enemy. Why, the Israelites didn't even have weapons until they disarmed their enemies. But what the Israelites did have was Deborah, a mighty smart leader who obeyed God by walking wherever He led her—even into battle. What a woman!

Perhaps you are feeling in the thick of things. Perhaps life has mounded up heaps of difficulties, and those around you are either reluctant to help, refuse to be part of the solution, or worse yet, are deliberately antagonistic toward you. Well, be of good cheer, for He who calls us to even the toughest assignments will also equip us with battle savvy. He will use His wisdom and our intelligence, His sovereignty and our circumstances, to strengthen our character and put a sweet song of victory on our lips. Now, that's food for thought.

On second thought, I don't think I've come far enough to have a tree named after me. What about a wildflower?

31

Resilient

*"The LORD sustains all who fall and raises
up all who are bowed down."*
(PSALM 145:14)

Synonyms: elastic, springy, rebounding

J've noticed that women who were held back in society
by financial limitations (Mary Hunt), physical disabilities
(Helen Keller), educational requirements (Harriet Tubman), or
prejudice (Rosa Parks) are often the ones who eventually lead
in one way or another. Instead of becoming bitter, they rely on
a higher government for the rulings in their lives, and they
become better, deeper, stronger, and sweeter. What others
would use against them, God uses in spite of us all. He has
given us a resilient nature and resilient minds so that, even if we
are pressed down, in His timing we will rise up.

Childbearing is one picture of a woman's resiliency, for
nothing is more pressing than labor, and yet we gals rise up
again after giving birth. I was certain during my first labor that
I could not crawl, much less walk.

And speaking of resilient, when I was about seven months
along, my rising tummy had stretched my skin so taut that I
thought I saw my baby smile at me in the mirror. My stretch
marks looked like a series of train tracks crisscrossing my

anatomy. Yet, when Marty was born, my body amazingly snapped back into shape. Okay, okay, maybe "snapped back" is a little optimistic, but it eventually did suck itself back into a form that no longer had to be housed under a gazebo cover.

Deborah was a mother and understood birth pains. Oh, I don't know if she birthed a baby, but I do know she arose as a mother in Israel. I know because she sang of it in her wonderful song after the battle. That's what mothers do; we sing to our children. We are known for our lullabies that quiet the colicky babe and nursery rhymes that entertain the child. And then we sing hymns that train and soothe the growing heart.

But Deborah's song was even more than that. It was a battle hymn and a victory chant. After witnessing God's awesome power, she employed her wits to come up with a song that she sang to high heaven. With the song, she hoped to tickle the memory of her children, the Israelites, so they would never

forget the Lord was the One who had fought their battle and had defeated their enemy.

Yes, just like a mom, Deborah wanted to create a mental picture that would help her kids understand lessons from life's circumstances. She reminded them that their obstinate hearts were responsible for bringing war to their city gates and that they didn't have as much as a shield or a spear among them to fight the enemy. Yes, just like a mom, she celebrated her children's resilient hearts when they finally decided to do the right thing. And yes, just like a mom, she reminded her children that whatever their position in life, whether as a traveler on a white donkey (rich) or traversing on foot (poor), they should lean in and listen to the songs at the watering places as they passed by. For there they would hear of the Lord's righteous acts.

The Song of Deborah is full of God's faithfulness. It also resounds with the human heart's resiliency. The Israelites were pressed down by their own sins, but when they listened to God's wisdom through their "mother's" lips, they arose to walk with the Lord again. How do we know this? Because of the sweetest words of all, found in one short, unforgettable sentence following the close of the song: "Then the land had peace forty years." Now that, my friends, is a lullaby.

Whatever your battle, regardless how formidable your enemy, God longs to bring you into the land of peace. Stand firm, walk faithfully, fight valiantly, sing to high heaven, and watch Him deliver you!

32

Intuitive

♥♡♥

*"I will give thanks to Thee, for I am fearfully
and wonderfully made."*
(PSALM 139:14)

Synonyms: instinctive, knowing, perceptive

hile I was browsing at the mall, an alarm was set off. Everyone in my vicinity turned to look in the direction of the sound, where we caught sight of a red-faced woman staring helplessly at her package. The clerk had failed to detach a sensor on the garments the shopper had purchased, resulting in the alarm being activated as she walked out of the store.

Being intuitive is like having an inside sensor. We women often sense things that sometimes go undetected by men, and usually our "sensing" is in regard to people. We often have a "knowing" about a person or situation we can't explain, but it's amazingly on target.

Now, please don't confuse intuitive with suspicious, for suspicion frequently is fueled by mistrust and resentment. Intuition is like a yellow light that alerts us to slow down and proceed cautiously or to take an alternate route.

Intuition goes beyond knowing, for knowing is based on gathered information, whereas intuition is based on something we don't fully understand and can't prove until after the fact.

Yet, when my intuitive button is pushed, it's like an inner store alarm chiming, reminding me to check my parcels carefully.

I would imagine that Deborah frequently had opportunity to use her intuitive nature as judge of her people. Sometimes people squabbled, but with a lack of hard facts to prove either side right, Deborah had to rely on her God-given gifts to determine a fair judgment.

In fact, isn't that what mamas often have to do with youngsters' battles and endless excuses? We turn on our sensors to decide if what we are hearing and seeing is accurate.

I remember how one day, when my eldest was a toddler, I walked through the room where he contentedly was playing. I glanced at him, but as I turned to walk away, my interior alarm went off. I didn't know why, but something didn't feel right. Sure enough, as I went back to investigate, I found an empty aspirin bottle shoved under the chair, the contents having been ingested by this complacent-looking cherub. Quick action coupled with a visit to the hospital remedied this near-disaster. But had I not responded to my intuition, I could have lost that precious parcel.

One friend told me she had a strong sense she needed to check on her toddler even though she had seen him only moments before. When she backtracked, she found her son headed pell-mell for a busy road.

We will never know how many tragedies have been averted because of women's sensors. I guess the Lord knew we would need to be equipped with this added perception.

My husband and I were introduced to a charismatic salesman who offered us the deal of a lifetime. He sounded good, he came with rave responses from mutual friends, and he appeared to be a solid believer. But something made me feel uneasy in his presence, so we kept our distance. Long story short, he turned out to be an impostor on all levels and took advantage of a lot of people.

Of course, sometimes we think we're responding to our intuition, but instead we're listening to our fearful side. My friend Ann tells of a time she was on a business trip and called home to check on her husband, Paul, and son, Rick. She knew they were attending a movie, what time they were going, and how long it would take to drive home. So she waited until they should have been home before she phoned. When no one answered, she wasn't concerned, thinking that perhaps they had stopped at the store for milk.

But when she rang the house again two hours later and still didn't get an answer, she panicked. First Ann called every hospital in the surrounding area. When that didn't turn up a lead, she called the police. She was so convinced of foul play or catastrophic accident that the police agreed to drive out to her country home while she sat in her hotel room and bawled. Fifteen minutes later, the phone rang. Paul chimed innocently, "Hi."

"'Hi'?!" Ann screamed. "'Hi'? Where have you been?!"

"The first showing was sold out, so we ate at a restaurant and then went to the late show," Paul reported calmly. Then he said, "Hold on. Someone's at the door." Ann remembered her call to the police and knew who was knocking. Quickly she told Paul she would talk to him later.

Ann has laughed many times since at that event and how she allowed her emotions, which were in overdrive, to career her imagination out of control. That's what we call having just enough information to make us dangerous. I've been there before. Again, this wasn't intuition; this was presumption. We need to be cautious because sometimes our emotional tendencies override our sensor. Then, instead of sensing, we are supposing, projecting, accusing, and imagining.

Sorting through female stuff can be so tricky. We don't want to miss the benefits of our built-in alarm systems, yet we don't want to act out of our insecurities and faulty humanity.

Experience will help to hone our sensor skills and teach us when it's intuition urging us to a certain action or our insecurities pulling us back. Heeding the admonition to be "quick to hear and slow to speak" will protect us from a pattern of over-reacting.

And if you have to ask yourself if your response is intuitive, it probably isn't. Intuition is just there; you just know to check on your child or to withhold your trust from someone. The dictionary uses words like "quick and ready insight; immediate apprehension or cognition" to describe intuition. The knowledge that something is true comes without bidding or working to come up with the information. Intuition can't be learned; either you have it or you don't. Many women do.

Intuition coupled with intellect, when our intellect is saturated in truth, is a powerful ally in a woman's life.

33

Intelligent

♥♡♥

"Speak, LORD, for your servant is listening."
(1 SAMUEL 3:9, NIV)

Synonyms: astute, discerning, smart

*S*ome of the smartest women I know have made some disastrous mistakes in their lives. Amazingly, those faux pas became the women's instructors, which caused them to expand and deepen intellectually. Some of us learn from our mistakes, while others run from them, failing to grasp the value packaged therein. Running almost always leaves one open to repeating foolish patterns for years to come. If you have made major blunders in your life (current or past), be of good cheer. They have the potential to make you one smart lady!

I find that heartening, for I, Mrs. Faux Pas herself, would like to believe that in my bulging bag of life's blunders nestles some shred of benefit for someone. If I poured out my bag's contents, you would see errors I made with my kids, unkind words I uttered to my husband, frittered opportunities, and frivolous financial decisions, to name a few boners. I'm grateful Jesus is our Redeemer, and He is able to take even our worst bunglings to teach us pertinent lessons. But we must linger in His counsel long enough to learn.

Proverbs is full of God's counsel—"smart bulletins"—alerting us to the importance of using our heads, as my dad would say, "for something other than a hat rack."

Solomon reminds us that, "The fear of the LORD is the beginning of knowledge" (Proverbs 1:7). Everything has a beginning, including knowledge. Recognizing who God is becomes the cornerstone for true intelligence. After all, it won't matter how many degrees we attain, how many people we impress with our wit and mental agility, or how many promotions we are awarded if we don't acknowledge God in all that we do. Without the fear of the Lord, all our efforts, however heroic, will be feeble and empty:

> For the LORD gives wisdom, and from his mouth come
> knowledge and understanding. He holds victory in store
> for the upright, he is a shield to those whose walk is
> blameless, for he guards the course of the just and pro-
> tects the way of his faithful ones (Proverbs 2:6-8, NIV).

As I read the above verses, I thought of Deborah and the battle she fought with the enemy. Her people didn't have weapons of warfare in a physical sense—no chariots, no swords, no shields. But their opponents had iron chariots, finely honed swords, and substantial shields.

I ask you, who in her right mind would want to take on vast troops of well-equipped soldiers itching to show off their superior position against a meager group (in comparison) of pipsqueaks co-led by a woman? Left to our own surmising, is there any doubt which side we would enlist with? Of course Sisera's army would be the reasonable choice.

But God's wisdom bypasses humankind's reasoning. We see God use torrents of rain as a shield for His people, and then we watch as the Lord guards and guides the Israelites into victory.

Deborah exhibited her intelligence when she chose to follow God's counsel regardless of the odds. Her insights obviously weren't controlled by her own genius, but instead she relied on God's wisdom to guide her into enlightened decisions.

Today we have that same opportunity when we fear the Lord and deliberately walk in His ways. For the times we fail miserably, we can learn from the Israelites, who, instead of running away from their problems, set aside their reluctant hearts, their disobedient ways, their past failures, and marched obediently into victory.

34

Steady

❤♡❤

"Oh, that my ways were steadfast ..."
(PSALM 119:5, NIV)

Synonyms: stable, consistent, unwavering, imperturbable

J find the word *steady* appealing. Just the thought of it helps to even out my Tigger disposition . . . or is that trigger disposition? I have to confess my emotions are not a well-kept secret. They tend to bound about for all to see. But sometimes (for micromoments) I've been the stabilizer in the midst of upheaval. Like the time some young people brought an injured, bleeding young man to me, and I quickly calmed the panicked group, called for emergency assistance—and then promptly turned 17 shades of green. My "steady" comes in short spurts. Oh, don't say spurts. That's what the young man's blood was doing from his torn vein. I'm grateful that we both recovered.

Because of my need to be more balanced, I selected the following life verse from Scripture: "He will be like a tree planted by the water that sends out its roots by the stream. It does not fear when the heat comes; its leaves are always green. It has no worries in a year of drought and never fails to bear fruit" (Jeremiah 17:8, NIV). For me, that verse is full of "steady." The tree doesn't flinch during the scorching sun, but continues to be green. It doesn't even give up when the sultry season turns into a devastating drought. In fact, that tree remains fruitful.

We see in Deborah's days that the heat of adversity came upon the people because of their willful acts of idolatry. Instead of drinking deeply from God's counsel, they followed their own lustful hearts, which caused the people to wither. Even their leaders shriveled up, and the result was a defenseless nation oppressed by its enemies.

Then along came Deborah, a woman who was sturdy in her faith, steady in God's ways, and ready to do what was asked of her. The result of Deborah's fruitful influence was triumph for an entire nation.

I'm certain Deborah was one of the "oaks of righteousness" that Isaiah speaks of when he refers to the "planting of the LORD" (Isaiah 61:3). Deborah stood tall like an oak deeply rooted in righteousness; she branched out in her faith, drawing others into the refreshing shade of truth; and she gave of the very fruit of her life to feed a famished people who had been too emaciated to fight their own battles.

I'm impressed. Of course, that's not the point of this account of Deborah's mindful service. Instead, we need to be inspired by this bright woman who used her faculties to honor God and benefit His people. We gals may have more emotions emitting per nanosecond than men, but that doesn't prevent us from being steady even in the midst of a drought. How many times have we heard it said by a grateful husband that his wife's unwavering faith pulled them through financial reversals, job losses, and other crises?

Yes, being balanced is an appealing quality, whether it's in reference to a sturdy ship on a storm-tossed sea, a steady oak in gale-force winds, or a ready woman in the upheaval of life.

35

Fruitful

❤♡❤

"The mind set on the Spirit is life and peace."
(Romans 8:6)

Synonyms: fertile, life-giving, plenteous

*H*ave you noticed how many artists paint bowls or baskets full of fruit? Apples, bananas, oranges, and grapes overflowing a woven container are visually pleasing. Actually, when you think about it, our minds are like containers, and what we place in them—our thoughts—determines the quality of our lives. When we think on things that are uplifting, kind, and wholesome, our minds become fruitful baskets. And that wholesome fruit nourishes our attitudes, desires, sense of well-being, relationships, and even our dreams.

It's up to us what we place in our minds, and it's a full-time occupation to root out unsavory thoughts. We are blitzed by the media, bombarded by worldly values, and exposed to violence and perversion. If that's not enough, we have our own vain imaginations to ward off. We need a filter, or as I once heard someone say, a phil-ter, based on the book of Philippians. If we establish a habit of phil-tering our thoughts through the good, true, pure, just, lovely, and good-repute sieve, it will assist us in attaining and maintaining sound mental health (see Philippians 4:8).

Mornings have been a lifetime challenge for me, as I tend to drag myself into a new day with some reluctance. I truly am grateful for being included in a new day once my pump is primed (my teeth are brushed, I'm dressed, and my bed is made, etc.). But getting through my regimen is a heavy chore when I lug my negativity around with me. To combat this mental habit of dreading to get going, I deliberately have worked to think of positive things at my first conscious stirrings. The moment my mind awakens, I begin to proclaim statements of gratitude. It's my way of offering a sacrifice of praise.

Sometimes I even sing in the morning, which, if you ever heard me, would cause you to increase your prayers on my family's behalf. It definitely isn't what I do best, but the thankful sounds help even my old, creaking bones to move with greater suppleness.

What a shame to miss out on joy in the early hours because we have failed to fill our baskets with notes of praise. Mornings are the gate into a brand-new day that the Lord has planned for us. Besides, our fruitful morning offerings please the Lord, He who is worthy of all our praise.

I find that if I ponder suspicious thoughts, I become mistrustful, insecure, and lonely. But when I direct my mind into fruitful thinking and consider God's faithfulness, I become trusting, secure, and confident. Thinking is one step away from becoming, and what is it we want to become? I think we would agree we want to be women of contentment, confidence, and character.

To assist in this outcome, let me suggest that we mentally plant a fruit-bearing tree in our backyard. Then we can engrave each fruit with a worthy consideration like forgiveness, purity, kindness, gentleness, encouragement, and compassion. The next time we begin to think in ways that damage relationships, rob us of our health, or cheat us out of our joy, we can go to our tree and pluck the healthy fruit of good thoughts and place them in the baskets of our minds.

I can't imagine how many times Deborah had to do that very thing to keep an honorable perspective. For she, too, lived in a sin-drenched society where even the leaders had fallen away as they worshiped other gods. But Deborah not only *had* a tree where people lined up to solve their disputes; she also *was* a tree (an oak of righteousness). And I believe she carefully filled her basket (mind) with virtuous thoughts. Deborah was a work of art. Proof of that is in the rich heritage she left behind for viewing by future generations.

36

Our Song to You: A Prayer

❤♡❤

$\mathcal{W}$hen I think on You, Lord, my inner life deepens, my life branches out, and my hope blossoms. How thrilling to know You have given us ways to strengthen our minds and then You use our mental capacities to bear fruitful results. We want to be Deborahs in our society and to use our mindset to address issues, whether they be a friend who needs godly counsel, a weakened leader who needs someone to come along beside, or a nation that needs a living example.

Help us to know the difference between Your gift of intuition and our tendency toward imagination. We want to be astute in holiness and of value to the cause of Christ. Steady us even in the midst of our daily battles with self-pity, skirmishes with others, and warfare against the evil one.

May You be pleased, Lord, with our thoughts, the content of our character, and the music generated from our hearts. We recognize that You have orchestrated our lives to have purpose and meaning. Our songs of victory, our shouts of praise, our hymns of faith are because of You . . . and only because of You. Amen.

A
WOMAN'S
HEART

37

Be My Valentine: The Shulammite Woman

❤♡❤

*I*n his day, King Solomon was a songwriter. I don't know if he made the top 10, but he composed 1,005 songs. Now that's prolific.

Recently I heard a well-known singer-writer interviewed. When he was asked which musical piece was his favorite, the gentleman pondered a moment and then answered, "It's sort of like children. One couldn't really pick one over another." Well, Solomon puts our minds to rest concerning his favorite by proclaiming it "Song of Songs," suggesting this surpassed all his other songs. I can almost guarantee it's Solomon's most romantic musical composition.

King Solomon collected wives like he wrote songs. His harems were bulging, which is probably why he wrote in Proverbs, "It is better to live in a corner of a roof, than in a house shared with a contentious woman" (Proverbs 21:9). There's nothing like firsthand experience, hey, king?

But when he sings of his bride in Song of Songs, we hear only the sweet notes and intimate exchange of two people who are head over heels in love. The tender names King Solomon and the Shulammite woman share with each other convey their deep feelings. In fact, Hallmark might want to check with this couple for card ideas, especially valentines. Here are just a few of their terms of endearment: beloved, lover, darling, bride, and the one my heart loves. Swoon. Isn't that valentine-ish? It makes my little ticker speed up.

I don't believe anything is more enhancing, thrilling, fulfilling, and satisfying for a woman than to know she is deeply loved by a man. Now, some of you may say, "Oh, thanks, Patsy. I'm single," or "I'm widowed," or "I'm married to Archie Bunker."

Well, that's what is so divine about this book of the Bible. While we observe the love between the king and his bride, we are being reminded of Christ's passionate love for each of us. He is our Bridegroom, and we are His bride. Christ longs to ease our fears and draw us into the safety of His loving presence. He romances our hearts with His love, and we have opportunity to respond with joy.

Take note of the Shulammite woman, for she had such ardent responses, and she felt such freedom to express her love. Her heart is open to her lover. Even though the song is sensual, it's also sacred in its spiritual content, which is why it's part of the Holy Writ.

We don't know the Shulammite woman's name. Perhaps we could call her Rose for this section of the book. Yes, Rose is fitting since she often visits her garden awaiting her lover. And he, too, refers to his beloved as a garden, a locked garden.

Rose and I invite you to take delight in the beauty of your feminine design and to bask in the understanding that you are truly loved. And best of all, God's love song to us is truly heart-warming.

38

Relational

"Eat, O friends, and drink; drink your fill, O lovers."
(SONG OF SONGS 5:1, NIV)

Synonyms: connection, communality, bond, rapport

I've observed that women's relational needs are stronger than men's. It's not that the men in our lives don't desire or need relationships, but they don't seem to require as many as we gals, nor do they expect as much out of relationships.

Someone asked my husband who his closest buddies were, and Les rattled off several names. Then he was asked the last time he called his pals on the phone just to see how they were. Answer: Never. Nor had his buddies called him. Yet they continue to consider themselves good friends.

Generally speaking, we gals don't operate that way. We chat, write, e-mail, fax, or telephone our closest relationships frequently. That's how we stay feeling connected. And for women . . . well, this woman anyway . . . connectedness is extremely important. We like to feel a part of our mates', our families', and our friends' lives. And because we tend to be more fluent, words form part of the glue that keeps us close.

One question I've heard women ask repeatedly about their husbands is "How do I get him to talk?" I've found that when

I'm quiet and not filling the air with words in an attempt to fill it for both of us, Les begins to chat. No, chatting really doesn't fit him. Perhaps conversing is a more accurate portrayal. I'm the chatterbox, or magpie, as my low-key dad often referred to me.

It's quite thrilling to know that Song of Songs was written by a man. King Sol was definitely a communicator. And he connected to Rose with a tenderness conveyed in breathtaking phrases. Listen as the king invites Rose into close relationship with him:

> Arise, my darling, my beautiful one, and come with me. See! The winter is past; the rains are over and gone. Flowers appear on the earth; the season of singing has come, the cooing of doves is heard in our land. The fig tree forms its early fruit; the blossoming vines spread their fragrance. Arise, come, my darling; my beautiful one, come with me (Song of Songs 2:10-13, NIV).

Pause and allow the beauty of that invitation to permeate your heart. Consider how our Lord woos us to enter His presence. He knows of our longings to relate with others, for He, too, longs to relate with us. He created us so that we might know Him and enjoy Him forever. In the Lord's presence it is eternal spring, fragrant and fruitful. And I find when I'm rightly connected to Christ, I'm able to relate with others more out of love than neediness. For in Christ's garden my icy heart melts and my inner blizzards still. That allows me to approach others without an agenda of needing them to meet my needs (which Christ never intended or designed them to do anyway).

I must confess that I have to be reminded regularly of these truths. My way is to run to flesh and blood to accomplish that which only God's Spirit can do in my heart: heal my hurts, lift my sadness, and dissolve my anger. My mate, family, and friends can be supportive, but they can't be the Spirit of the Lord, the Lover of my soul.

I love spring, the season of hope. I love the smell of spring, fragrant with blossoms. I love the look of spring, alive with promise. And most of all, I love Him who designed spring, giving us an unforgettable picture of the newness of life. May we turn toward spring and thereby turn toward the Lord, who shelters us throughout all the seasons of our lives.

39

Romanticist

♥♡♥

"Many waters cannot quench love; rivers cannot wash it away."
(SONG OF SONGS 8:7, NIV)

Synonyms: idealist, rhapsodist, sentimentalist

I'm a sentimental kind of gal who loves moonlight, candlelight, and the flickering light of a fireplace. I enjoy the way music gentles the atmosphere and softens one's attitude. I appreciate a lovely food presentation (especially if someone else is cooking). And I'm wild about unexpected small remembrances—a handwritten love note, a photograph, a favorite shared song, a hand-drawn piece of art, a personalized poem, an old locket. I'm into romantic walks, hand holding, and shared secrets. And don't forget a fistful of violets, an armload of hydrangeas, or a solitary rose. Ah, love.

I think most women savor intimate moments. Well, ladies, I don't know when you last strolled through the Song of Songs, but it sizzles with love's dynamics. This book overflows with the sights and sounds of romance, full of dreamy word pictures that cause a girl to swoon. Listen: "My lover is to me a sachet of myrrh resting between my breasts" (1:13, NIV). What I hear this love-struck woman saying is that her sweetheart's scent pleases her, and she wants always to hold him close to her heart. Rose also mentions, "His left arm is under my head, and his right arm embraces me" (2:6, NIV). Not only is this an intimate embrace, but it's a secure position, one where she feels safe and cared for. I like that.

Her beloved tells Rose, "Your voice is sweet, and your face is lovely" (2:14, NIV). He delights in how she sounds and how she looks. "How beautiful you are, my darling! Oh, how beautiful!" (1:15, NIV). He really does appreciate Rose's appearance; note the exclamation marks that emphasize his feelings. These two people are thrilled with each other and are prepared to tell the world.

When I met my husband I was only 15, but I was certain of my feelings for this rascally, romantic 16-year-old. I showed his picture to all my friends and stared at it starry-eyed for endless hours. I watched the mailbox vigilantly and treasured every word he wrote.

Another Man is in my life whom I also treasure. I love the sound of His name . . . Jesus. When I met Him, I couldn't wait to tell others of this One who passionately cared for me. I began to search the love letter of His Word, resting my eyes on His expressions of acceptance of me. I read and reread that Jesus loved me, He loved me, He loved me. He found my voice sweet as I spoke to Him in prayer, and He found my face lovely as I looked up to Him. The Lord promises to always hold me near, which causes me to feel safe in His love.

Yes, girls, there's nothing like being romanced. And to imagine that our Beloved is a Prince. No, make that *the* Prince, and of great importance to us, He is *our* Prince. He has waited for us, searched for us, and longed for our company. He is the Rose of Sharon and the Lily of the Valley. He brings us the sweet fragrance of hope. Ah, love—pure, holy love.

40

Lovely

♥♡♥

"You have stolen my heart with one glance of your eyes."
(SONG OF SONGS 4:9, NIV)

Synonyms: engaging, rapturous, alluring

To be lovely means we have beauty that's emotionally appealing as well as visually pleasing. Visually, huh? Well, if you don't count the first hour after I crawl out from between rumpled sheets, and if we hit a rare day when my hair is cooperating and my sinuses aren't acting up, leaving me sniffy and swollen, then I'm kind of cute. But lovely? That would be a stretch. Although there have been moments. . . .

About six years ago I was in my friend's wedding as her matron of honor for a December ceremony. The bride had selected scrumptious, long, black-velvet dresses for us, with mutton sleeves, high-collared necks, and Victorian lace in a V on the front. We carried white lanterns encircled with flowers and lit with pink tapers. The sanctuary was aglow in tiny white Christmas lights wrapped in tulle and appeared to be a storybook setting for a prince and princess.

On this rare occasion, every hair on my head knew what it was supposed to do and actually did it. My dress had been altered and fit just the way I had hoped it would. I felt lovely.

Sometimes I treat myself to a manicure, a pedicure, and a shoulder massage. That's usually good for, oh, two hours of lovely. Then I chip a nail and my neck kinks up. I've found beauty is fleeting if we count strictly on outward appearance.

Although, ladies, I must say after my last stroll through the grocery store that we can do better than we are. I know it's tempting, especially on busy days, to dash out to the store hoping we won't bump into anyone who matters. But the reality for those of us who love Christ is that in God's economy, everyone matters. It takes only a minute to tidy our hair, apply a little lip color and fresh deodorant, and to make sure our garments are clean and, for heaven's sake, fit appropriately.

If lovely is more than touching up our makeup before we head out to snatch that carton of milk, what is emotionally pleasing beauty? Well, I know that when I'm feeling good about who I am, I tend to get more compliments on how I look. I also know that we can behave in certain ways that cause people to say, "Isn't she a lovely person."

That comment is usually made about genteel women who graciously extend themselves to others. Their speech is seasoned

liberally with words that communicate interest, concern, and support: "May I help?" "I'm so sorry." "Here, allow me." "Please take my place." "You matter to me."

We read in Song of Songs that Rose was a lovely, dark-skinned woman. Solomon was so smitten with her loveliness that he promised to have gold earrings studded with silver made for her. (Hmm, nice move, king.) Rose tells us of how her perfume drew the king's interest, and how he was like a cluster of scented blossoms from the vineyards.

There is something so lovely when we emit fragrance—the fragrance of Christ. When we purpose to spend time with our first love, we become aware of the precious aroma of His presence. And because we have breathed in the intoxicating fragrance of His love, we emit loveliness—emotionally appealing and visually pleasing loveliness.

Rose thought of her beloved as she arose. She searched for him throughout the day and watched eagerly for him in the evening. And she valued him more than silver or gold. Obviously Rose's heart was focused on the love of her life. Is ours?

41

Springtime Love:
A Prayer

♥♡♥

*Y*ou have filled Your Word with music and invited us to joyously enter into songs of praise, adoration, and jubilation. You have even offered to put new songs on our lips, verses we have not yet sung. But may we remember also to listen and hear the words You sing to us through Scripture and through Your Holy Spirit.

As You, Lord, romance us with Your stunning love, may You find us, Your bride, receptive and eager for Your company. Because we've been so disappointed in others, we've become practiced at walking in the chilly winds of winter that leave our words biting and our hearts bitter. May we discard our heavy apparel and clothe ourselves in garments of celebration.

You have called us to arise, to leave winter behind, and to enter the springtime of Your love. Take our hand, Beloved, for we are frail, but we want to become fruitful, like a garden, a vineyard, a field of lilies. And, Lord, we want to be faithful to You, our first love. Amen.

A Woman's Spirit

42

Sing a Zestful Song: Miriam

❤♡❤

*M*iriam, a spirited young girl, watched carefully to see her baby brother's fate. She and her mom, Jochebed, had placed the baby into a basket and slipped him into the crocodile-infested Nile to protect him from the slaughter of Hebrew male children taking place in Egypt. When an Egyptian princess found the wee child bobbing in the baby ark, her heart was moved to compassion.

That was when Miriam went into action. She appeared before the princess and offered to find a Hebrew nurse to care for little Moses until he was weaned. The princess accepted the offer, and Miriam scurried to fetch her mom. Soon baby and mother were reunited, thanks to God's sovereign design and young Miriam's courage.

Imagine a slave girl of 12 approaching the enemy's princess and having the poise to convincingly present her plan. Miriam's little heart must have been pounding wildly in her chest. And think of her joy, as she dashed to tell her mom what God had done for them. I can picture Miriam and Jochebed hugging, laughing, crying, and dancing around the room in celebration and gratitude.

After young Moses was moved to the palace to be raised, we don't hear about Miriam again for 80 years. We know she and her brother Aaron remained in Egypt as slaves, praying for a deliverer. Miriam's life was hard; much was expected of her. But when Moses was sent by Jehovah God to lead His people out of captivity, Moses chose his sister to be chief singer. She still, even after mistreatment by cruel taskmasters, had a song in her heart. Miriam was in her 90s by that time and obviously had a lot of spirit to lead the Hebrew women in music and dance.

While Moses made Miriam a music leader, the Lord called her to be a leader in proclaiming truth, for we are told she was a prophetess. After eight decades of separation, this sister and her two brothers, Moses and Aaron, were reunited to lead God's people to the Promised Land. What an incredible calling. God prepared each of them—Miriam, Moses, and Aaron—for such a time as this.

Somewhere, though, in the 40-year desert trek through the scorching heat, with obstinate people, in the face of formidable enemies, Miriam's joyful song turned to a dirge. In the last years of her life, we find our spirited sister in a struggle—a power struggle with the Almighty. The Lord disciplined her, which broke her body and her spirit. Miriam died just before the people entered into the Promised Land.

Come join me as we take Miriam's hand. She has come a long way across the sea, around the mountains, and through enemy territory. She has known hunger, thirst, and humiliation. Miriam's story is important for us because she demonstrates the honorable use of her gifts, she exemplifies courage, and she illustrates long-suffering. She also prompts us to celebrate before the Lord with thanksgiving. And lastly, she reminds us of the dangers of growing old and cold in our spirits. A temptation, dear sisters, we will all eventually face.

43

Enthusiastic

♥♡♥

"Sing and make music in your heart to the Lord."
(Ephesians 5:19, NIV)

Synonyms: zealous, ardent, eager

I appreciate enthusiastic people, those who click their heels and boogie through life with color and flair. Even their fingerprints sparkle as they touch our lives in vivid ways.

My friend Shirley is like that. Everywhere she goes, people are warmed, entertained, motivated, and blessed. Even now, as lively memories of her twirl through my mind, I have to giggle.

Shirley can take an ordinary task and turn it into an unforgettable event. She loves to have fun and has a tiny tendency toward . . . uh, disaster. What starts out simple can become cataclysmic in a short time, which truthfully is one of her endearing qualities. The sound of her generous laughter never fails to draw people in, and her ability to laugh at herself makes her everyone's friend.

Throughout our long friendship we have had many an adventure together—from women's retreats, to family parties, to shopping extravaganzas, to moving expeditions, to church events. You can always be assured that if Shirley is involved, the ordinary glitters with the promise of surprise.

Shirley does everything with her enthusiasm throttle wide open. When she serves others, she does so with verve; when she entertains, she does so with artistry; when she sings, she does so with gusto. Why, even her dress is chic and lively. She's an ornate gal whose hallmarks are her charm and her color. She sports a half dozen rings on her fingers, multiple bracelets dangle from her wrists, several necklaces drape her throat, generous earrings drip from her lobes, and she tops it all off with a sassy hat tipped to one side. Go, girlfriend!

And get this: Shirley was my pastor's wife (still is his wife). Don't you love it! Think how easy it would have been for Shirley to stuff her flair in an attempt to fit others' expectations. Instead, she has added pizzazz wherever she has gone.

But I believe Shirley has nothing on Miriam. I mean, imagine 92-year-old Miriam picking up tambourines and leading the nation's women in dance and song. Now, that's exciting. I know a few in that age bracket who could pick up the tambourines, but to be the lead dancer and singer of a nation? I don't think so.

And picture this: Miriam still had 40 years of hotfooting it across the desert ahead of her, not to mention her leadership role over hundreds of thousands of women. Yes, Miriam was one spunky lady.

It's a shame when we face life with a colorless attitude. And believe me, I've been stuck in beige, dreading to face each day. Auntie Mame, in her earthy way, enthusiastically declared, "Life is a banquet, and most poor suckers are starving to death."

The word *enthusiasm* means "God within," and that means no one should be more electrified by life than Christians. C'mon, girls. Let's pick up the tambourines and live our lives with zippity-doo-dah. Anyone can do dull. It takes a "God within" person to dance and sing before the nation and, more importantly, before our Lord.

44

Leader

❤♡❤

"Teach me your way, O LORD; lead me in a straight path."
(PSALM 27:11, NIV)

Synonyms: guide, boss, supervisor

I'm bossy. There, I said it. Others—actually multitudes—have suggested this is true of me. I, of course, let them know in no uncertain terms that they were wrong. So there.

I have learned and continue to learn that "bossy" under the Holy Spirit's protection and correction is a good thing. Wouldn't you know it; now that I've grasped this insight, I'm not nearly as bossy as I once was. That's because I've become so indecisive; I can't make up my mind what to be bossy about.

Most leaders are bossy. The great leaders are so good at bossing that others don't realize they've been bossed. It comes off more as a directional gift: This is the way; walk ye in it. I have to believe that in 40 years of wandering, as the leader of the Israelite women, Miriam had to do a lot of directing: "Hey, you by the camel, move over with the others by the well."

All kidding aside, Miriam directed them in worship and celebration and also in their daily living, for she was a prophetess. A prophetess was a woman who heard from God on a regular basis and instructed others in His paths: This is the way; walk ye in it.

Hmm, Miriam is reminiscent of Old Testament Deborah, who also served as a leader, a prophetess, and a singer. The major difference between the two seems to be the last chapter of their lives. We left Deborah singing a victory chant, followed by 40 years of peace, whereas Miriam, after 40 years of disruption, has lost her song. Let's see why.

Moses, her famous brother, married a woman outside of the Hebrew nation, and sister Miriam was not a happy camper. As a matter of fact, Miriam was ready to pull up her tent pegs and clobber her younger brother. She was so angered that she was prepared to head up an insurrection against Moses' leadership. She wasn't prepared for the anger God rained on her pompous parade.

We need to trade in our bossy combat boots for delicate ballet slippers when it comes to stepping into God's established territory. And Moses' leadership position was definitely God's call. Remember the bush? Well, Miriam became a bush—a tumbleweed. She withered and was an outcast after the Lord God disciplined her inappropriate and unacceptable behavior with leprosy. How frightening, and how humiliating for this ancient woman of God.

The Israelites were as devastated as her brothers. Moses and Aaron fell on their faces before the Lord in behalf of their sister, pleading for her restoration. The nation sat in sorrow over the outcome of Miriam's mutiny. The Hebrew people agreed not to move on without their beloved leader and friend. What an impact her life must have had to create that kind of loyalty and devotion. Imagine an entire nation in mourning and in agreement to wait it out for one person. I'm impressed.

I'm also depressed. This once-spirited leader was relegated to sitting well outside the camp, and crying, "Unclean! Unclean!" That breaks my heart. But I'm grateful God mercifully restored Miriam's health and allowed her to return to her people. We hear no more about this humbled leader until her burial. It's as if the experience of excommunication erased her irascible energy. Then again, perhaps during her misery Miriam promised the Lord that if He healed her, she wouldn't be bossy or bitter, but would live and lead quietly for the remainder of her days.

None of us knows how many days we have been allotted— but surely not as long as Miriam (132 years). I'm relieved about that, for I have a feeling the longer I hang around here, the more susceptible I am to becoming a tumbleweed.

45

Forgiven

"Forgive my hidden faults."
(Psalm 19:12, NIV)

Synonyms: pardoned, acquitted, released

When I was a young girl, I wanted to grow up to be a newspaper reporter. Today, as an un-young girl, I still imagine myself from time to time clicking pictures of noteworthy folks and scribbling down important details. If I had been assigned to cover Miriam, I wonder how I would have framed this famed woman.

I would have definitely started with shots at the Nile. Click. I hope I would have captured the suspense and concern on young Miriam's face. Click, click. And I wouldn't have missed the jubilation when baby Moses, Mama, and daughter were reunited. Here I would have noted the inexpressible emotional bond between a woman and her child. I would have reported on the tears of gratitude and relief that poured from Jochebed's eyes, spilling onto the baby's face, washing away his fear (or so I imagine). Click.

I would have been at Miriam's side when she was reunited with her brother Moses as adults. Click. Did they laugh? Cry? Feel awkward? Did they shake hands, hug, or swap sandals?

And don't think for a moment that I would have missed the Red Sea extravaganza. Talk about a photo op! That would have taken at least a few rolls. Click, click, click.

Then I would have reloaded quickly when the celebration began and the women worshiped in song and dance with Miriam leading in these joyous moments. Click, click.

I'm not sure how many camels I'd have needed to tote all my film. I mean, 40 years of clicking could be exhausting, but the outcome would be thrilling. I would have photographed Miriam's sandals, her tambourines, and of course her tent. (We all like to see each other's homes. Right, girls?) Click.

I don't know if Miriam used her gift of prophecy at large outdoor assemblies, old-fashioned tent gatherings, or informal campfire circles, but I'd have been there taking snapshots. I would have followed Miriam throughout her day, capturing her involvement with the women. Click. I'd film her meetings with her brother Aaron as they reported to Moses regarding their responsibilities (the heads of state).

But I don't know if I would have had the heart to snap a picture of Miriam, Mama of the Desert, when she was twisted with deforming leprosy. Miriam's dejection would have caused me, I'm sure, to turn away so as not to add to her despair. Besides, we would rather not be reminded of some moments, especially in living color.

The most dramatic moments in Miriam's history, I believe, would have been when she was forgiven, physically healed, and restored to her people. Click, click, click. I'm sure many tears of gratitude were shed when she stepped back into the camp and into the lives of those who still loved her dearly.

Miriam must have been startled to see her body grotesquely covered in ulcerated sores one moment and fully restored the next. It's much like when we are aware of our own filthy guilt one moment. Then the next moment, we take in God's forgiveness. He cleanses our ulcerated heart and straightens our twisted life, and we're left breathless. Such cleansing fills us with relief, rekindles our hope, and humbles us. Yes, to be forgiven is humbling. Deeply, deeply, humbling. Ask Miriam. Click.

46

Spirited Offering: A Prayer

❤♡❤

*F*ather, we Your children are in need of Your forgiveness. Without it we will remain so full of ourselves that we will be of little value to anyone else. And our spirits will wither without Your life-giving presence. One word from You and we, too, like Miriam, will be able to enter back into life with humbled hearts of hope.

Each day You give to us is a gift. May we unwrap it with zeal, wear it with style, and celebrate it with gratitude. Increase our enthusiasm, for then even the ordinary becomes spectacular.

Spirited women easily run amok. So we pray, Lord, that You would renew a steadfast spirit within us. We desire to live with purpose and direction, being willing to take direction as well as offer it.

We pray that it delights You when we enter Your presence with a spirit of jubilation. We offer up our alleluias and our songs to You, who guides us along valley floors, over mountaintops, and across desert sands. May we not hesitate to follow Your lead.

Enliven our leadership so that we might offer prophetic utterances—not our opinions, but Your unalterable truth. Color our beige spirits with Your radiant presence so that others will be drawn to the dazzling Christ in us. Amen.

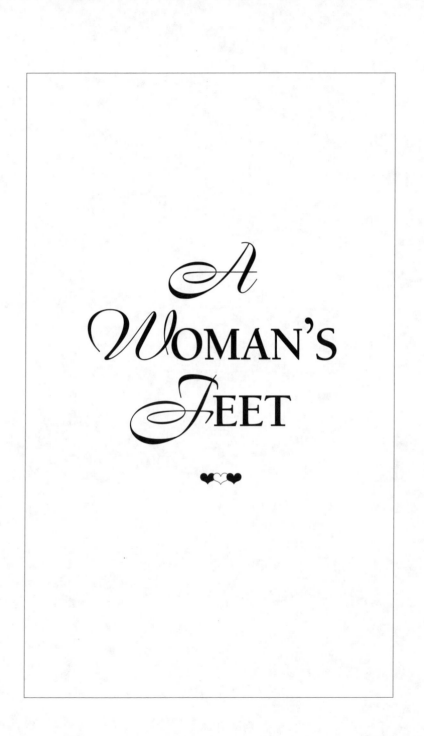

47

Two Paths to Travel: Mary of Bethany

❤♡❤

$\mathcal{T}$he path of life is seldom without ups, downs, and turn-arounds. In fact, I find some days I skip along merrily with my hair dancing in the breeze, while other days I drag my sorry self about as if I'm carrying the weight of the world in my backpack. Between the breezy days and the backpack days are the endless brick-carrying days, which seem to be how I spend the majority of my time. My brick days are the times I purpose to put one foot in front of the other, taking care to do the tasks at hand. I choose on those days to believe that the discipline as well as the drudgery fit into a higher destiny, that the bricks of obedience and follow-through serve a greater purpose than just to give me an aerobic workout.

The problem with transporting bricks is that we are so busy with the lifting and the carrying that we catch only glimpses of the progress. Perhaps that is as it was meant to be, lest we become so impressed with our little stack of bricks that we distract ourselves from the higher calling, which is to add our bricks to the tried-and-true paths laid by those who have gone before us. This task is for our benefit and for those who will follow after us.

After all, there is nothing like a well-ordered, well-lit, well-marked path. Ask Mary of Bethany.

Mary, sister of Martha, seems inseparable from her sibling; each time we read of one sister, we hear of the other. Well, almost every time. For instance, remember when the brick path led to their doorway, and the duo entertained Jesus and His disciples in their home? Martha felt put upon because, while she was saddled with all the chores, Mary was seated at Jesus' feet. What a to-do that caused! I mean, folks have been finger-pointing at the sisters ever since, picking sides over who was right and who was wrong. Should Mary have helped Martha prepare for their guests, or should Martha have been sitting next to Mary at the Savior's feet?

Hmm, I just wonder if they both weren't doing the right thing. Perhaps their portrait paints for us two necessary paths that are often women's to walk in: one of physical leadership and service and one of spiritual availability and responsiveness. Of course, the challenge is figuring out when to walk each path in life's fullness.

Mary seemed certain of her calling in regard to Jesus. We see that her footpath led her repeatedly to His feet. That's where we find her sitting, weeping, kneeling, listening, and ever questioning. Life's demands were not about to vie for Mary's attention. Somehow she sensed her time to be with the Savior was now. Jesus acknowledged her wisdom and affirmed her decisions. How deeply satisfying that must have been.

I want to be a Mary, yet I also need to be a Martha. She was busy with many things, which is true for most of us. We are called to be responsible for the tasks at hand, yet we long to be spiritually responsive to the Lord. So must we give up one path to follow the other—or is it possible these two paths converge at certain points?

I believe we can pace our race. Not easy, but possible. It takes determination to pick up one foot and put it in front of the other without forsaking the sitting-at-His-feet time. In the pages ahead, we will slip into Mary's sandals and walk her purposed path in hopes that we, too, will know the sweetness of His approval while doing our part to leave a clear path.

48

Faithful

♥♡♥

"Well done, good and faithful servant!"
(MATTHEW 25:21, NIV)

Synonyms: loyal, devoted, incorruptible

*T*ravel can be frustrating. I'm sure this isn't a news flash, especially to those of you who frequent the freeways and airways. Out there we encounter accidents, road repairs, equipment problems, rush-hour snarls, weather-related delays, and people glitches.

Since I'm a regular trotter across our great nation, I'm accustomed to detours of all types. Usually I handle these well, but sometimes when my cup is tipped, what pours out isn't . . . uh, sweet. I believe our walk and our talk reveal our faithfulness— or lack thereof—and the content of our hearts. Our outer reactions to life magnify, for everyone's viewing pleasure, our inner condition.

Now, women often display faithfulness, even with tipped cups. They are loyal to friends and family, sometimes to a fault, as they overlook the shortcomings of their loved ones. Women express devoted enthusiasm and support of those in their lives. And they believe betrayal of a friendship is a high crime. I adhere to all these tenets of faithfulness, but I don't always live like I do.

Last week, when I arrived at the ticket counter and was told my flight was canceled, I was disappointed. I was booked on another airline and had only 20 minutes to make the plane. While dragging my three pieces of luggage past 25 gates, I began to develop a 'tude. But it really expanded when I arrived breathless at the boarding gate and was told they could check my baggage only halfway. Then I would have to retrieve it myself in Dallas, haul it to another terminal, and then sprint (ha!) to my connecting flight.

As displeased as I was, I held my tongue. But as my flight taxied, my thoughts began to soar. No, make that "roar." I began to quarrel mentally with everyone I had encountered and might encounter on this trek—including the Lord. Talk about a breeding ground for ill will. I wasn't responding like a faithful follower of Christ, but more like a mumbling lost soul.

You see, I had this trip figured out. I had pictured myself arriving at the airport, boarding my plane, flying to my destination, and arriving rested from the quiet sky hours. I believed that once I had done my part, everyone involved would be faithful to do his or her part. Instead, not only did my trip go awry, but I also robbed myself of rest because of the mental racket in my head.

Between pretending to tell off the airlines, I did manage to come up with Plan B, which was to grab a skycap as soon as I landed to help me take my luggage to the other terminal. But when I arrived at baggage claim, I found that this airport used skycaps for check-in passengers only. So I rented a cart, loaded my luggage, and hotfooted it to the tram. But when I tried to push the cart onto the tram, the wheels jammed, and my stuff and I were wedged in the closing doorway. A pilot riding the tram came to my rescue, pulling my cart and me safely aboard. After I smoothed my ruffled appearance and thanked the helpful pilot, I confessed to him, "I'm too little to travel alone."

Ever feel that way? That life is too much? The trips too treacherous? That people can't be counted on to faithfully do their part? That we don't have the ability to faithfully do ours?

I wonder if that's how Mary felt when her life went terribly awry. Her brother, Lazarus, had died, and even though we all expect people to die, we never are prepared when it's our loved ones. Even when they have lived a long time, if they aren't suffering, we want them to live longer yet. It's only human nature.

When Mary and her sister had time to think about their loss, they believed that had Jesus been there, their brother wouldn't have died. How they must have faithfully held one another, consoled each other, and devoted hours to helping each other right their tipped cups. The mental anguish of thinking about how differently this could have turned out was at the forefront of their minds. We know that, for when Jesus arrived, the sisters both expressed this to Him. In fact, Mary fell to His feet in tears.

Life seldom unfolds for us without obstacles, snags, hindrances, and inconveniences. Some are as simple as changed travel plans and some as devastating as the loss of a loved one. Understanding that we are not victims of a world careening out of control, but that our footsteps are safely guided by a sovereign and faithful God, will ease our struggle. He has not lost track of us. He is not surprised by our hardships. He knew our way would be formidable. He told us so.

There is good news about our sometimes poor reactions, those unfaithful moments: When we see our inner condition, it can become our most valuable insight on how to pray for ourselves. Also, it can be a reminder of our need to pray for others who have been unfaithful in some way toward us. And at those moments, we often have faithful women, ever present and loyal, to help us through our tipped-cup times. I'm grateful the Lord understands our frailty, our faultiness, and our fears, and faithfully receives us—even with our tears.

I want to become a woman who, when my cup is tipped by life's inequities, spills out faith.

49

Foundational

❤❤

"He set my feet on a rock and gave me a firm place to stand."
(PSALM 40:2, NIV)

Synonyms: base, support, footing

*F*eet are foundational. Ask my husband, Les, who is struggling to save his feet from diabetes's ravages. Then, while fighting for his footing, he fell, resulting in an explosive breaking of bones, which complicated his health issues.

Through the past few years, we have learned in our home how vital feet are to one's mobility. Les has been on crutches, in casts, on canes, and more recently he's been a gadabout in his motorized cart. As helpful as all those support systems are, he says they don't compare to standing up and walking across the room on one's two feet.

Feet are odd fellows. They come in so many shapes (wide, narrow, lumpy) and varying sizes. I wear a five-and-a-half shoe, which is mammoth next to my mom's size four. But my shoe looks childlike next to my husband's extra-wide size 11. Have you noticed how yummy baby's feet are, while oldsters' feet are so feetlike?

What in the world happens to the appearance of a person's feet as she racks up miles? Seems as though they expand, and the toes begin to do funny things, like curl. Hmm, what's that about? Also, toenails thicken and discolor (Ew!). What purpose does that serve? Our heels take on the appearance of pumice stones and pull unsightly snags in our pantyhose. Who needs that? I don't know about you, but when I'm on my feet a lot, or I wear the wrong shoes, I get cramps the size of Nebraska in my toes.

Yep, feet are foundational, and their condition profoundly impacts our daily lives. Recently, my friend Sheila Walsh presented me with some Scottish foot cream called "My Dogs Are Barking." The name made me giggle because plenty of times my barking dogs have set me on the sidelines, times when I felt as though I couldn't take another step.

I remember one weary trip on which I removed my high heels in the Dallas airport as I hiked from one gate to another. I was convinced my departing gate was in Oklahoma as I trudged down the endless concourses. Finally a driver stopped his cart and told me to get in. Trust me, he didn't have to repeat the offer. When I made it home, dogs still howling, I burned the high heels.

Mary of Bethany, I'm certain, wore more foundational footgear than *moi*. No spike sandals in her wardrobe; she didn't want anything impeding her progress. She seemed to understand that if she were to be a woman who could walk down the endless concourses of life, she must kneel, rest, and learn at Jesus' feet while there was yet time to do so. Mary didn't know while she knelt that, after the Lord's death, she could still sit quietly at His feet in meditative moments; that He would meet with her in quiet hours as well as turbulent times just as surely as He did when He walked the earth; that He longed to continue to make Himself known in the dailyness of her walk and to direct her feet onto right paths. What a relief it must have been the first time, after Christ's resurrection, that she encountered

Him during her private prayers. Or found Him her faithful companion through life's trials as He filled her mind with His words and comforted her heart with the Holy Spirit.

We have that same opportunity for foundational faith. Even during our barking-dog days, the Lord woos us to sit at His feet and learn of Him. We, in turn, can bring the quiet and peace we receive at Jesus' feet and lay it at the feet of our families. I believe women are an important part of their family's security. When it is well in our hearts, a sense of safety permeates our entire household. It's like the revealing quote, "When Mama ain't happy, ain't nobody happy." So whether we wear a size-four shoe or a size 11; whether we are an EEE or a DD width; whether we Reebok down life's path or wheelchair it; what truly makes us capable of marching on is faith in Christ Jesus.

50

Follower

*"[Christ left] you an example,
that you should follow in His steps."*
(1 PETER 2:21, NIV)

Synonyms: disciple, pupil, devotee

*T*hrough the years, my friend Lana and I frequently have found ourselves roommates as we minister together. This match is similar to Laverne and Shirley or Felix and Oscar, the Odd Couple. We, like them, are extremely different.

Lana likes the room chilled until ice chips flake off the mirrors, whereas I prefer the meltdown approach; when the light fixtures begin to dissolve, I dial down. Lana is up and down all night long, like Wee Willie Winkie. I, on the other hand, expire each evening and don't resurrect until daylight fills the room. Then I come forth like Lazarus, the look of pallor across my face. Lana is quiet by nature, while I am . . . oh, never mind; you get the idea.

But one quality we share is that neither of us has a clue as to our whereabouts most of the time. When we head out for the day, Lana almost always takes the lead, and I almost always follow at her heels. Instead of stepping into the elevator, invariably we slam into the soda pop machine at the opposite end of the hall. It's not Lana's fault, for she is the first to tell me not to follow her. But my forgetter forgets. She walks with such confidence that I always believe Lana knows where she is going. I've learned, after repeated cola-can-shaped bruises on my forehead, to make sure I follow someone who knows where she is going.

One of the funniest runarounds I experienced was when my husband and I followed my parents on some back roads in Kentucky. My dad, famous for shortcuts, was certain he remembered from his childhood a quick way to arrive at my aunt's home. As roads narrowed and homes disappeared, we were sure he had missed a turn. Suddenly a one-lane bridge was before us. We inched across the rickety structure and found ourselves encircled by abandoned mines. For some reason, this struck Les and me as funny, and we laughed until we cried. My dad didn't find it that amusing, which added to our enjoyment.

In a world that insists we should be leaders, being a follower holds little appeal, much less humor. Yet that is exactly what the Lord calls us to be. In the world's eyes, to be a follower suggests weakness, but in God's government it proves wisdom.

Mary of Bethany never measured taller than when she was at Jesus' feet. She was His follower during celebration, devastation, and grief. Even when she didn't understand the Lord's ways, she knelt in His presence. And when she knew the Lord would leave this earth, she acquiesced in humbleness and followed His servant example by anointing His sweet feet. Her sensitivity, generosity, and devotion are moving.

I purposed in my heart to follow Jesus many years ago. I wish that I could tell you I've been consistent in that attempt. But sometimes I've followed my own counsel, which led me into the desert. I have followed the crowd, which led me to wide, barren places. I have followed the popular belief of the day, which led to imbalance.

But every time I wandered, the Lord came for me and

guided me back onto the right path, where He once again offered to lead. I'm so grateful He didn't laugh at my lostness or leave me abandoned.

Oh, merciful Jesus, may I be sensitive enough, generous enough, and devoted enough to follow You, and only You, all the days of my life.

51

Footpath to the Lord: A Prayer

♥♡♥

*T*hank You, Lord, that You didn't leave a bread-crumb trail for us to try to follow to find our way through the maze of this life. Instead, You left indelible footprints, the lantern of Your Word, and Your promise always to go before us.

It comforts and encourages us, Lord, to see that You met Mary in her home and in her heartbreak. You, Man of Sorrows, resurrected her joy. Come this day into our homes. We welcome You. And into our heartbreak. We need You.

Teach us to be Marys, for she faithfully followed You and honored You by listening closely, learning deeply, and loving unselfishly. Shoe our feet with willing obedience so that we, too, might walk in Your ways. Amen.

I Love Being a Woman

♥♡♥

*W*hat an incredible journey we have taken with our sisters, from Sarah to Ruth to Deborah to the Shulammite woman. We've slipped into their sandals and followed them into their homes, their workplaces, and even into enemy territory. These champions of the faith, through hardships and heartbreak, have become our heroines, for they remind us that we aren't alone in our struggles. We realize that they, too, wrestled with their emotions. They were "feeling women" who learned, sometimes the hard way, not to allow their emotions to dictate their behavior.

Remember Sarah's snit fit? I've had those, not for the same reason, but nonetheless I've overreacted, which caused people around me to take cover. Of course, I've had Deborah moments as well, fleeting as they may have been—moments in which I stayed steady, fought bravely, and sang of God's victory. Then, when I remember the mix of tenderness Ruth extended to her mother-in-law, blended with the courage she exhibited as she walked away from everything she had ever known, I'm heartened. Yes, I've been encouraged as I've examined these ladies' lives.

And I've needed that encouragement. A couple of years ago, Les and I found a Southwest desert nest to move into for the cold months of Michigan's winter. This allowed Les to benefit physically in his battle against severe health issues, and it provided me a place to write with minimal interruptions. What I hadn't anticipated was my struggle with placement. I was more than homesick; I suffered a mini-crisis trying to figure out where I fit into this new setting with its cactuses, scorpions, earthquakes, and walled neighborhoods. The differences between Michigan's winter wools and California's cool cottons were compounded by my need to feel a part of my surroundings.

In the midst of my adjustment, I thought of Sarah's radical adjustments as she left everything she had known to follow her husband to who-knows-where. No wonder she was cranky. I thought of Abigail, who suddenly found herself residing in the king's quarters (lovely, yet odd). Also aging Miriam, who spent the last 40 years of her life pulling up stakes (how disruptive), and Ruth, who wholeheartedly followed God's lead after losing so much.

What a reminder for me that my security is in Christ, not Michigan; a Savior, not a setting. (The Shulammite woman could have given me lessons worth learning on love.) The Lord would lead me in this new land I found myself in just as surely as He guided Esther out of her fear and into her future, facing it with courage.

Once I relaxed in His care, I began to see things differently. I became more aware of the desert's sunsets, mountains, palm trees, and generous portions of sunlight. I learned that I tend to depend on my outer surroundings to give me a sense of safety and placement.

Mentally, I know that Christ is our security, whether we are in a palace or a pasture, on a pinnacle or in a pit. Yet emotion-ally I feel fragile at times, longing for tangible comforts. That's why, girlfriends, it's so helpful to have the saints of old and our sisters of today, whom we can gain insights from as we observe their devotion to Christ at all costs. May we remember Mary of Bethany, who positioned herself at Christ's feet so that He might lift her up. Each of these women in the Bible spurs us to look forward to the days ahead with greater vision, just as the Proverbs 31 woman would urge us to. For even if God leads us to a desert, He will continue to work in us and through us.

Being a woman is thrilling, emotions and all, but it doesn't mean we will always do the right thing in this life. In fact, we're guaranteed we will be indulgent, independent (in a heady way), and insolent. We need each other's rubber-band examples of failure and fame to learn how to handle all aspects of life with greater dignity and to become emotionally healthy women.

Never underestimate the beauty of your feminine design. The Lord created us to exhibit grace, strength, and softness, and to articulate sensitive intelligence. What a privilege! What a joy!

I love being a woman!

Celebration

I love being a woman.
It's really quite a thrill
to know that I'll be bounding
hormonally uphill.
That is, until I'm 50,
when the elevator stops,
and I lose my concentration
as my estrogen level drops.
Oh, my head's still on my shoulders
but my cells have slipped a bit,
which leaves me perplexed
and given to little snit fits.
That's when I run to my Father
to give me what I need.
He guides me to a narrow path
where He offers to lead.
So if you are a woman,
rejoice at your design.
Your image has been fashioned
with your future in His mind.
Celebrate your purposes
and live out your life
with joy, peace, and hope
in the midst of stress and strife.
Yes, I love being a woman,
hormones, perplexed, and all,
and I'll stay on His path—
I just hope we pass a mall!

Take a Lighthearted Look at Life . . .

with these other books by Patsy Clairmont!

God Uses Cracked Pots

How does God best reveal Himself in us? When we allow His light to shine through the broken places of our lives. With many hilarious and a few embarrassing tales of a self-proclaimed "cracked pot," Patsy Clairmont encourages readers to take themselves a little less seriously and enjoy life to the fullest, as He intended. Paperback and book-on-cassette.

Normal Is Just a Setting on Your Dryer

All of us have things about ourselves that we're not too crazy about. But once we start the comparison game, we wind up in an endless cycle that leaves us all wet! Packed with more of Patsy's side-splitting stories and anecdotes, this best seller is perfect for anyone stuck in the rut of trying to measure up. Paperback and book-on-cassette.

Sportin' a 'Tude

Patsy's back, and she's better than ever! And readers will be smiling in agreement as she takes a good look at our attitudes and what they communicate to others. In her typical honest, light-hearted manner, Patsy reveals the many ways our attitudes speak volumes—*especially* when we're not looking—to point us toward the one 'tude we should display: the attitude of Christ. Paperback and book-on-cassette.

. . .

Look for these books in your favorite Christian bookstore. You can also request a copy by calling 1-800-A-FAMILY or by writing Focus on the Family, Colorado Springs, CO 80995. Friends in Canada may call 1-800-661-9800 or write Focus on the Family, P.O. Box 9800, Stn. Terminal, Vancouver, B.C. V6B 4G3. Visit our Web site—www.family.org—to learn more about the ministry or to find out if there is a Focus on the Family office in your country.

subject to availability

FOCUS ON THE FAMILY®

Welcome to the Family!

Whether you received this book as a gift, borrowed it from
a friend, or purchased it yourself, we're glad you read it! It's just
one of the many helpful, insightful, and encouraging
resources produced by Focus on the Family.

In fact, that's what Focus on the Family is all about—providing inspira-
tion, information, and biblically based advice to people in all stages of life.

It began in 1977 with the vision of one man, Dr. James Dobson, a licensed
psychologist and author of 16 best-selling books on marriage, parenting,
and family. Alarmed by the societal, political, and economic pressures
that were threatening the existence of the American family, Dr. Dobson
founded Focus on the Family with one employee—an assistant—
and a once-a-week radio broadcast, aired on only 36 stations.

Now an international organization, Focus on the Family is dedicated
to preserving Judeo-Christian values and strengthening the family
through more than 70 different ministries, including eight separate
daily radio broadcasts; television public service announcements;
11 publications; and a steady series of award-winning books,
films, and videos for people of all ages and interests.

Recognizing the needs of, as well as the sacrifices and important
contribution made by, such diverse groups as educators, physicians,
attorneys, crisis pregnancy center staff, and single parents,
Focus on the Family offers specific outreaches to uphold and
minister to these individuals, too. And it's all done for one purpose,
and one purpose only: to encourage and strengthen individuals
and families through the life-changing message of Jesus Christ.

• • •

For more information about the ministry, or if we can be of help to your
family, simply write to Focus on the Family, Colorado Springs, CO 80995
or call 1-800-A-FAMILY (1-800-232-6459). Friends in Canada may write
Focus on the Family, P.O. Box 9800, Stn. Terminal, Vancouver, B.C. V6B 4G3
or call 1-800-661-9800. Visit our Web site—www.family.org—
to learn more about the ministry or to find out if there is a
Focus on the Family office in your country.

We'd love to hear from you!